ON MURDER CONSIDERED AS ONE OF THE FINE ARTS

THOMAS DE QUINCEY

FV EDITIONS

CONTENTS

FIRST PAPER ON MURDER,
CONSIDERED AS ONE OF THE
FINE ARTS.

TO THE EDITOR OF
BLACKWOOD'S MAGAZINE.   3
LECTURE.   6

SECOND PAPER ON MURDER,
CONSIDERED AS ONE OF THE
FINE ARTS.   51
THREE MEMORABLE MURDERS.   76
*A SEQUEL TO 'MURDER CONSIDERED AS
ONE OF THE FINE ARTS.*

FIRST PAPER ON MURDER, CONSIDERED AS ONE OF THE FINE ARTS.

TO THE EDITOR OF
BLACKWOOD'S MAGAZINE.

(1827)

Sir,—We have all heard of a Society for the Promotion of Vice, of the Hell-Fire Club, &c. At Brighton, I think it was, that a Society was formed for the Suppression of Virtue. That society was itself suppressed—but I am sorry to say that another exists in London, of a character still more atrocious. In tendency, it may be denominated a Society for the Encouragement of Murder; but, according to their own delicate [Greek: euphaemismos], it is styled—The Society of Connoisseurs in Murder. They profess to be curious in homicide; amateurs and dilettanti in the various modes of bloodshed; and, in short, Murder-Fanciers. Every fresh atrocity of that class, which the police annals of Europe bring up, they meet and criticise as they would a picture, statue, or other work of art. But I need not trouble myself with any attempt to describe the spirit of their proceedings, as you will collect that much better from one of the Monthly Lectures read before the society last year. This has fallen into my hands accidentally, in spite of all the vigilance exercised to keep their transactions from the public eye. The publication of it will alarm them; and my purpose is that it should. For I would much rather put them down quietly, by an appeal to public opinion through you, than by such an exposure of names as would follow an appeal to Bow Street; which last appeal, however, if this should fail, I must positively resort to. For it is scandalous that such things should go on in a Christian land. Even in a heathen land, the toleration of murder was felt by a Christian writer to be the most crying reproach of the public morals. This writer was Lactantius; and with his words, as singularly applicable to the present occasion, I shall conclude: "Quid tam horribile," says he, "tam tetrum, quam hominis trucidatio? Ideo severissimis legibus vita nostra munitur; ideo bella execrabilia sunt. Invenit tamen consuetudo quatenus homicidium sine bello ac sine legibus faciat: et hoc sibi voluptas quod scelus vindicavit. Quod si interesse homicidio sceleris conscientia est,—et eidem facinori spectator obstrictus est cui et admissor; ergo et in his gladiatorum cædibus non minus cruore profunditur qui spectat, quam ille qui facit: nec potest esse immunis à sanguine qui voluit effundi; aut videri non interfecisse, qui interfectori et favit et proemium postulavit." "Human life," says he, "is guarded by laws of the uttermost rigor, yet custom has devised a mode of evading them in behalf of murder; and the demands of taste (voluptas) are now become the same as those of abandoned guilt." Let the Society of Gentlemen Amateurs consider this; and let me call their especial attention to the last sentence, which is so weighty, that I shall attempt to convey it in English: "Now, if merely to be present at a murder fastens on a man the character of an accomplice; if barely to be a spectator involves us in one common guilt with the perpetrator; it follows of necessity, that, in these murders of the amphitheatre, the hand which inflicts the fatal blow is not more deeply imbrued in blood than his who sits and looks on: neither can *he* be clear of blood who has countenanced its shedding; nor that man seem other than a participator in murder who gives his applause to the murderer, and calls for prizes in his behalf." The "*præmia postulavit*" I have not yet heard charged upon the Gentlemen Amateurs of London, though undoubtedly their proceedings tend to that; but the "*interfectori favil*" is implied in the very title of this association, and expressed in every line of the lecture which I send you.

I am, &c. X. Y. Z.

LECTURE.

Gentlemen,—I have had the honor to be appointed by your committee to the trying task of reading the Williams' Lecture on Murder, considered as one of the Fine Arts; a task which might be easy enough three or four centuries ago, when the art was little understood, and few great models had been exhibited; but in this age, when masterpieces of excellence have been executed by professional men, it must be evident, that in the style of criticism applied to them, the public will look for something of a corresponding improvement. Practice and theory must advance pari passu. People begin to see that something more goes to the composition of a fine murder than two blockheads to kill and be killed—a knife—a purse—and a dark lane. Design, gentlemen, grouping, light and shade, poetry, sentiment, are now deemed indispensable to attempts of this nature. Mr. Williams has exalted the ideal of murder to all of us; and to me, therefore, in particular, has deepened the arduousness of my task. Like Æschylus or Milton in poetry, like Michael Angelo in painting, he has carried his art to a point of colossal sublimity; and, as Mr. Wordsworth observes, has in a manner "created the taste by which he is to be enjoyed." To sketch the history of the art, and to examine its principles critically, now remains as a duty for the connoisseur, and for judges of quite another stamp from his Majesty's Judges of Assize.

Before I begin, let me say a word or two to certain prigs, who affect to speak of our society as if it were in some degree immoral in its tendency. Immoral! God bless my soul, gentlemen, what is it that people mean? I am for morality, and always shall be, and for virtue and all that; and I do affirm, and always shall, (let what will come of it,) that murder is an improper line of conduct, highly improper; and I do not stick to assert, that any man who deals in murder, must have very incorrect ways of thinking, and truly inaccurate principles; and so far from aiding and abetting him by pointing out his victim's hiding-place, as a great moralist [1] of Germany declared it to be every good man's duty to do, I would subscribe one shilling and sixpense to have him apprehended, which is more by eighteen-pence than the most eminent moralists have subscribed for that purpose. But what then? Everything in this world has two handles. Murder, for instance, may be laid hold of by its moral handle, (as it generally is in the pulpit, and at the Old Bailey;) and that, I confess, is its weak side; or it may also be treated æsthetically, as the Germans call it, that is, in relation to good taste.

To illustrate this, I will urge the authority of three eminent persons, viz., S.T. Coleridge, Aristotle, and Mr. Howship the surgeon. To begin with S.T.C. One night, many years ago, I was drinking tea with him in Berners' Street, (which, by the way, for a short street, has been uncommonly fruitful in men of genius.) Others were there besides myself; and amidst some carnal considerations of tea and toast, we were all imbibing a dissertation on Plotinus from the attic lips of S.T.C. Suddenly a cry arose of "Fire—fire!" upon which all of us, master and disciples, Plato and [Greek: hoi peri ton Platona], rushed out, eager for the spectacle. The fire was in Oxford Street, at a piano-forte maker's; and, as it promised to be a conflagration of merit, I was sorry that my engagements forced me away from Mr. Coleridge's party before matters were come to a crisis. Some days after, meeting with my Platonic host, I reminded him of the case, and begged to know how that very promising exhibition had terminated. "Oh, sir," said he, "it turned out so ill, that we damned it unanimously." Now, does any man suppose that Mr. Coleridge,—who, for all he is too fat to be a person of active virtue, is undoubtedly a worthy Christian,—that this good S. T. C., I say, was an incendiary, or capable of wishing any ill to the poor man and his piano-fortes (many of them, doubtless, with the additional keys)? On the contrary, I know him to be that sort of man, that I durst stake my life upon it he would have worked an engine in a case of necessity, although rather of the fattest for such fiery trials of his virtue. But how stood the case? Virtue was in no request. On the arrival of the fire-engines, morality had devolved wholly on the insurance office. This being the case, he had a right to gratify his taste. He had left his tea. Was he to have nothing in return?

I contend that the most virtuous man, under the premises stated, was entitled to make a luxury of the fire, and to hiss it, as he would any other performance that raised expectations in the public mind, which afterwards it disappointed. Again, to cite another great authority, what says the Stagyrite? He (in the Fifth Book, I think it is, of his Metaphysics) describes what he calls [Greek: kleptaen teleion], i.e., a perfect thief; and, as to Mr. Howship, in a work of his on Indigestion, he makes no scruple to talk with admiration of a certain ulcer which he had seen, and which he styles "a beautiful ulcer." Now will any man pretend, that, abstractedly considered, a thief could appear

to Aristotle a perfect character, or that Mr. Howship could be enamored of an ulcer? Aristotle, it is
well known, was himself so very moral a character, that, not content with writing his
Nichomachean Ethics, in one volume octavo, he
also wrote another system, called Magna Moralia,
or Big Ethics. Now, it is impossible that a man
who composes any ethics at all, big or little,
should admire a thief per se, and, as to Mr. Howship, it is well known that he makes war upon all
ulcers; and, without suffering himself to be se-
duced by their charms, endeavors to banish them
from the county of Middlesex. But the truth is,
that, however objectionable per se, yet, relatively
to others of their class, both a thief and an ulcer
may have infinite degrees of merit. They are both
imperfections, it is true; but to be imperfect being
their essence, the very greatness of their imperfection becomes their perfection. Spartam nactus es,
hunc exorna. A thief like Autolycus or Mr. Bar-
rington, and a grim phagedænic ulcer, superbly
defined, and running regularly through all its natural stages, may no less justly be regarded as
ideals after their kind, than the most faultless
moss-rose amongst flowers, in its progress from
bud to "bright consummate flower;" or, amongst
human flowers, the most magnificent young female, apparelled in the pomp of womanhood.
And thus not only the ideal of an inkstand may be
imagined, (as Mr. Coleridge demonstrated in his

celebrated correspondence with Mr. Blackwood,) in which, by the way, there is not so much, because an inkstand is a laudable sort of thing, and a valuable member of society; but even imperfection itself may have its ideal or perfect state.

Really, gentlemen, I beg pardon for so much philosophy at one time, and now let me apply it. When a murder is in the paulo-post-futurum tense, and a rumor of it comes to our ears, by all means let us treat it morally. But suppose it over and done, and that you can say of it,[Greek: Tetelesai], or (in that adamantine molossus of Medea) [Greek: eirzasai]; suppose the poor murdered man to be out of his pain, and the rascal that did it off like a shot, nobody knows whither; suppose, lastly, that we have done our best, by putting out our legs to trip up the fellow in his flight, but all to no purpose—"abiit, evasit," &c.—why, then, I say, what's the use of any more virtue? Enough has been given to morality; now comes the turn of Taste and the Fine Arts. A sad thing it was, no doubt, very sad; but we can't mend it. Therefore let us make the best of a bad matter; and, as it is impossible to hammer anything out of it for moral purposes, let us treat it æsthetically, and see if it will turn to account in that way. Such is the logic of a sensible man, and what follows? We dry up our tears, and have the satisfaction, perhaps, to discover that a transaction, which, morally considered, was shocking, and without a leg to stand upon, when tried by principles of Taste, turns out to be a very meritorious performance. Thus all the world is pleased; the old proverb is justified, that it is an ill wind which blows nobody good; the amateur, from looking bilious and sulky, by too close an attention to virtue, begins to pick up his crumbs, and general hilarity prevails. Virtue has had her day; and henceforward, Vertu and Connoisseurship have leave to provide for themselves. Upon this principle, gentlemen, I propose to guide your studies, from Cain to Mr. Thurtell. Through this great gallery of murder, therefore, together let us wander hand in hand, in delighted admiration, while I endeavor to point your attention to the objects of profitable criticism.

~

The first murder is familiar to you all. As the inventor of murder, and the father of the art, Cain must have been a man of first-rate genius. All the Cains were men of genius. Tubal Cain invented tubes, I think, or some such thing. But, whatever were the originality and genius of the artist, every art was then in its infancy, and the works must be criticised with a recollection of that fact. Even Tubal's work would probably be little approved at this day in Sheffield; and therefore of Cain (Cain senior, I mean,) it is no disparagement to say, that his performance was but so so. Milton, however, is supposed to have thought differently. By his way of relating the case, it should seem to have been rather a pet murder with him, for he re-touches it with an apparent anxiety for its picturesque effect:

> Whereat he inly raged; and,
> as they talk'd,
> Whereat he inly raged; and,
> as they talk'd,
> Smote him into the midriff
> with a stone
> That beat out life: he fell; and,
> deadly pale,
> Groan'd out his soul *with
> gushing blood effus'd.*
> *Par. Lost, B. XI.*

Upon this, Richardson, the painter, who had an eye for effect, remarks as follows, in his Notes on Paradise Lost, p. 497: "It has been thought," says he, "that Cain beat (as the common saying is) the breath out of his brother's body with a great stone; Milton gives in to this, with the addition, however, of a large wound." In this place it was a judicious addition; for the rudeness of the weapon, unless raised and enriched by a warm, sanguinary coloring, has too much of the naked air of the savage school; as if the deed were perpetrated by a Polypheme without science, premeditation, or anything but a mutton bone. However, I am chiefly pleased with the improvement, as it implies that Milton was an amateur. As to Shakspeare, there never was a better; as his description of the murdered Duke of Gloucester, in Henry VI., of Duncan's, Banquo's, &c., sufficiently proves.

The foundation of the art having been once laid, it is pitiable to see how it slumbered without improvement for ages. In fact, I shall now be obliged to leap over all murders, sacred and profane, as utterly unworthy of notice, until long after the Christian era. Greece, even in the age of Pericles, produced no murder of the slightest merit; and Rome had too little originality of genius in any of the arts to succeed, where her model failed her. In fact, the Latin language sinks under the very idea of murder. "The man was murdered;"—how will this sound in Latin? Interfectus est, interemptus est—which simply expresses a homicide; and hence the Christian Latinity of the middle ages was obliged to introduce a new word, such as the feebleness of classic conceptions never ascended to. Murdratus est, says the sublimer dialect of Gothic ages. Meantime, the Jewish, school of murder kept alive whatever was yet known in the art, and gradually transferred it to the Western World. Indeed the Jewish school was always respectable, even in the dark ages, as the case of Hugh of Lincoln shows, which was honored with the approbation of

Chaucer, on occasion of another performance from the same school, which he puts into the mouth of the Lady Abbess.

Recurring, however, for one moment to classical antiquity, I cannot but think that Catiline, Clodius, and some of that coterie, would have made first-rate artists; and it is on all accounts to be regretted, that the priggism of Cicero robbed his country of the only chance she had for distinction in this line. As the subject of a murder, no person could have answered better than himself. Lord! how he would have howled with panic, if he had heard Cethegus under his bed. It would have been truly diverting to have listened to him; and satisfied I am, gentlemen, that he would have preferred the utile of creeping into a closet, or even into a cloaca, to the honestum of facing the bold artist.

To come now to the dark ages—(by which we, that speak with precision, mean, par excellence, the tenth century, and the times immediately before and after)—these ages ought naturally to be favorable to the art of murder, as they were to church architecture, to stained glass, &c.; and, accordingly, about the latter end of this period, there arose a great character in our art, I mean the Old Man of the Mountains. He was a shining light, indeed, and I need not tell you, that the very word "assassin" is deduced from him. So keen an amateur was he, that on one occasion, when his own life was attempted by a favorite assassin, he was so much pleased with the talent shown, that notwithstanding the failure of the artist, he created him a duke upon the spot, with remainder to the female line, and settled a pension on him for three lives. Assassination is a branch of the art which demands a separate notice; and I shall devote an entire lecture to it. Meantime, I shall only observe how odd it is, that this branch of the art has flourished by fits. It never rains, but it pours. Our own age can boast of some fine specimens; and, about two centuries ago, there was a most brilliant constellation of murders in this class. I need hardly say, that I allude especially to those five splendid works,—the assassinations of William I, of Orange, of Henry IV., of France, of the Duke of Buckingham, (which you will find excellently described in the letters published by Mr. Ellis, of the British Museum,) of Gustavus Adolphus, and of Wallenstein. The King of Sweden's assassination, by the by, is doubted by many writers, Harte amongst others; but they are wrong. He was murdered; and I consider his murder unique in its excellence; for he was murdered at noon-day, and on the field of battle,—a feature of original conception, which occurs in no other work of art that I remember. Indeed, all of these assassinations may be studied with profit by the advanced connoisseur. They are all of them *exemplaria,* of which one may say,—

Nociurnâ versatâ manu, ver-
sate diurne;
Especially *nocturnâ.*

In these assassinations of princes and states-
men, there is nothing to excite our wonder; important changes often depend on their deaths; and,
from the eminence on which they stand, they are
peculiarly exposed to the aim of every artist who
happens to be possessed by the craving for
scenical effect. But there is another class of assassinations, which has prevailed from an early period
of the seventeenth century, that really does surprise me; I mean the assassination of philoso-
phers. For, gentlemen, it is a fact, that every
philosopher of eminence for the two last centuries
has either been murdered, or, at the least, been
very near it; insomuch, that if a man calls himself
a philosopher, and never had his life attempted,
rest assured there is nothing in him; and against
Locke's philosophy in particular, I think it an
unanswerable objection (if we needed any), that,
although he carried his throat about with him in
this world for seventy-two years, no man ever
condescended to cut it. As these cases of philoso-
phers are not much known, and are generally
good and well composed in their circumstances, I
shall here read an excursus on that subject, chiefly
by way of showing my own learning.

The first great philosopher of the seventeenth

century (if we except Galileo) was Des Cartes; and if ever one could say of a man that he was all but murdered—murdered within an inch—one must say it of him. The case was this, as reported by Baillet in his *Vie De M. Des Cartes*, tom. I. p. 102-3. In the year 1621, when Des Cartes might be about twenty-six years old, he was touring about as usual, (for he was as restless as a hyæna,) and, coming to the Elbe, either at Gluckstadt or at Hamburgh, he took shipping for East Friezland: what he could want in East Friezland no man has ever discovered; and perhaps he took this into consideration himself; for, on reaching Embden, he resolved to sail instantly for West Friezland; and being very impatient of delay, he hired a bark, with a few mariners to navigate it. No sooner had he got out to sea than he made a pleasing discovery, viz. that he had shut himself up in a den of murderers. His crew, says M. Baillet, he soon found out to be "des scélérats,"—not amateurs, gentlemen, as we are, but professional men—the height of whose ambition at that moment was to cut his throat. But the story is too pleasing to be abridged; I shall give it, therefore, accurately, from the French of his biographer: "M. Des Cartes had no company but that of his servant, with whom he was conversing in French. The sailors, who took him for a foreign merchant, rather than a cavalier, concluded that he must have money about him. Accordingly they came to a resolution by no means advantageous to his purse. There is this difference, however, between sea-robbers and the robbers in forests, that the latter may, without hazard, spare the lives of their victims; whereas the other cannot put a passenger on shore in such a case without running the risk of being apprehended. The crew of M. Des Cartes arranged their measures with a view to evade any danger of that sort. They observed that he was a stranger from a distance, without acquaintance in the country, and that nobody would take any trouble to inquire about him, in case he should never come to hand, (quand il viendroit à manquer.") Think, gentlemen, of these Friezland dogs discussing a philosopher as if he were a puncheon of rum. "His temper, they remarked, was very mild and patient; and, judging from the gentleness of his deportment, and the courtesy with which he treated themselves, that he could be nothing more than some green young man, they concluded that they should have all the easier task in disposing of his life. They made no scruple to discuss the whole matter in his presence, as not supposing that he understood any other language than that in which he conversed with his servant; and the amount of their deliberation was—to murder him, then to throw him into the sea, and to divide his spoils."

Excuse my laughing, gentlemen, but the fact is, I always do laugh when I think of this case—two things about it seem so droll. One, is, the horrid panic or "funk," (as the men of Eton call it,) in which Des Cartes must have found himself upon hearing this regular drama sketched for his own death—funeral—succession and administration to his effects. But another thing, which seems to me still more funny about this affair is, that if these Friezland hounds had been "game," we should have no Cartesian philosophy; and how we could have done without that, considering the worlds of books it has produced, I leave to any respectable trunk-maker to declare.

However, to go on; spite of his enormous funk, Des Cartes showed fight, and by that means awed these Anti-Cartesian rascals. "Finding," says M. Baillet, "that the matter was no joke, M. Des Cartes leaped upon his feet in a trice, assumed a stern countenance that these cravens had never looked for, and addressing them in their own language, threatened to run them through on the spot if they dared to offer him any insult." Certainly, gentlemen, this would have been an honor far above the merits of such inconsiderable rascals —to be spitted like larks upon a Cartesian sword; and therefore I am glad M. Des Cartes did not rob the gallows by executing his threat, especially as he could not possibly have brought his vessel to port, after he had murdered his crew; so that he must have continued to cruise for ever in the Zuyder Zee, and would probably have been mistaken by sailors for the Flying Dutchman, homeward bound. "The spirit which M. Des Cartes manifested," says his biographer, "had the effect of magic on these wretches. The suddenness of their consternation struck their minds with a confusion which blinded them to their advantage, and they conveyed him to his destination as peaceably as he could desire."

Possibly, gentlemen, you may fancy that, on the model of Cæsar's address to his poor ferry-man,—"Cæsarem vehis et fortunas ejus"—M. Des Cartes needed only to have said,—"Dogs, you cannot cut my throat, for you carry Des Cartes and his philosophy," and might safely have defied them to do their worst. A German emperor had the same notion, when, being cautioned to keep out of the way of a cannonading, he replied, "Tut! man. Did you ever hear of a cannon-ball that killed an emperor?" As to an emperor I cannot say, but a less thing has sufficed to smash a philosoper; and the next great philosopher of Europe undoubtedly was murdered. This was Spinosa.

I know very well the common opinion about him is, that he died in his bed. Perhaps he did, but he was murdered for all that; and this I shall prove by a book published at Brussels, in the year 1731, entitled, La Via de Spinosa; Par M. Jean Colerus, with many additions, from a MS. life, by one of his friends. Spinosa died on the 21st February, 1677, being then little more than forty-four years old. This of itself looks suspicious; and M. Jean admits, that a certain expression in the MS. life of him would warrant the conclusion, "que sa mort n'a pas été tout-à-fait naturelle." Living in a damp country, and a sailor's country, like Holland, he may be thought to have indulged a good deal in grog, especially in punch,[2] which was then newly discovered. Undoubtedly he might have done so; but the fact is that he did not. M. Jean calls him "extrêmement sobre en son boire et en son manger." And though some wild stories were afloat about his using the juice of mandragora (p. 140,) and opium, (p. 144,) yet neither of these articles appeared in his druggist's bill. Living, therefore, with such sobriety, how was it possible that he should die a natural death at forty-four? Hear his biographer's account:—"Sunday morning the 21st of February, before it was church time, Spinosa came down stairs and conversed with the master and mistress of the house." At this time, therefore, perhaps ten o'clock on Sunday morning, you see that Spinosa was alive, and pretty well. But it seems "he had summoned from Amsterdam a certain physician, whom," says the biographer, "I shall not otherwise point out to notice than by these two letters, L.M. This L.M. had directed the people of the house to purchase an ancient cock, and to have him boiled forthwith, in order that Spinosa might take some broth about noon, which in fact he did, and ate some of the old cock with a good appetite, after the landlord and his wife had returned from church.

"In the afternoon, L.M. staid alone with Spinosa, the people of the house having returned to church; on coming out from which they learnt, with much surprise, that Spinosa had died about three o'clock, in the presence of L.M., who took his departure for Amsterdam the same evening, by the night-boat, without paying the least attention to the deceased. No doubt he was the readier to dispense with these duties, as he had possessed himself of a ducatoon and a small quantity of silver, together with a silver-hafted knife, and had absconded with his pillage." Here you see, gentlemen, the murder is plain, and the manner of it. It was L.M. who murdered Spinosa for his money. Poor S. was an invalid, meagre, and weak: as no blood was observed, L.M., no doubt, threw him down and smothered him with pillows,—the poor man being already half suffocated by his infernal dinner. But who was L.M.? It surely never could be Lindley Murray; for I saw him at York in 1825; and besides, I do not think he Would do such a thing; at least, not to a brother grammarian: for you know, gentlemen, that Spinosa wrote a very respectable Hebrew grammar.

Hobbes, but why, or on what principle, I never could understand, was not murdered. This was a capital oversight of the professional men in the seventeenth century; because in every light he was a fine subject for murder, except, indeed, that he was lean and skinny; for I can prove that he had money, and (what is very funny,) he had no right to make the least resistance; for, according to himself, irresistible power creates the very highest species of right, so that it is rebellion of the blackest die to refuse to be murdered, when a competent force appears to murder you. However, gentlemen, though he was not murdered, I am happy to assure you that (by his own account) he was three times very near being murdered. The first time was in the spring of 1640, when he pretends to have circulated a little MS. on the king's behalf, against the Parliament; he never could produce this MS., by the by; but he says that, "Had not his Majesty dissolved the Parliament," (in May,) "it had brought him into danger of his life." Dissolving the Parliament, however, was of no use; for, in November of the same year, the Long Parliament assembled, and Hobbes, a second time, fearing he should be murdered, ran away to France. This looks like the madness of John Dennis, who thought that Louis XIV. would never make peace with Queen Anne, unless he were given up to his vengeance; and actually ran away from the sea-coast in that belief. In France, Hobbes managed to take care of his throat pretty well for ten years; but at the end of that time, by way of paying court to Cromwell, he published his Leviathan. The old coward now began to "funk" horribly for the third time; he fancied the swords of the cavaliers were constantly at his throat, recollecting how they had served the Parliament ambassadors at the Hague and Madrid. "Turn," says he, in his dog-Latin life of himself,

> "Tum venit in mentem mihi
> Dorislaus et Ascham;
> Tanquam proscripto terror
> ubique aderat."

And accordingly he ran home to England. Now, certainly, it is very true that a man deserved a cudgelling for writing Leviathan; and two or three cudgellings for writing a pentameter ending so villanously as—"terror ubique aderat!" But no man ever thought him worthy of anything beyond cudgelling. And, in fact, the whole story is a bounce of his own. For, in a most abusive letter which he wrote "to a learned person," (meaning Wallis the mathematician,) he gives quite another account of the matter, and says (p. 8,) he ran home "because he would not trust his safety with the French clergy;" insinuating that he was likely to be murdered for his religion, which would have been a high joke indeed—Tom's being brought to the stake for religion.

Bounce or not bounce, however, certain it is, that Hobbes, to the end of his life, feared that somebody would murder him. This is proved by the story I am going to tell you: it is not from a manuscript, but, (as Mr. Coleridge says,) it is as good as manuscript; for it comes from a book now entirely forgotten, viz., "The Creed of Mr. Hobbes Examined; in a Conference between him and a Student in Divinity," (published about ten years before Hobbes's death.) The book is anonymous, but it was written by Tennison, the same who, about thirty years after, succeeded Tillotson as Archbishop of Canterbury. The introductory anecdote is as follows: "A certain divine, it seems, (no doubt Tennison himself,) took an annual tour of one month to different parts of the island. In one of these excursions (1670) he visited the Peak in Derbyshire, partly in consequence of Hobbes's description of it. Being in that neighborhood, he could not but pay a visit to Buxton; and at the very moment of his arrival, he was fortunate enough to find a party of gentlemen dismounting at the inn door, amongst whom was a long thin fellow, who turned out to be no less a person than Mr. Hobbes, who probably had ridden over from Chattsworth. Meeting so great a lion,—a tourist, in search of the picturesque, could do no less than present himself in the character of bore. And luckily for this scheme, two of Mr. Hobbes's companions were suddenly summoned away by express; so that, for the rest of his stay at Buxton, he had Leviathan entirely to himself, and had the honor of bowsing with him in the evening.

Hobbes, it seems, at first showed a good deal of stiffness, for he was shy of divines; but this wore off, and he became very sociable and funny, and they agreed to go into the bath together. How Tennison could venture to gambol in the same water with Leviathan, I cannot explain; but so it was: they frolicked about like two dolphins, though Hobbes must have been as old as the hills; and "in those intervals wherein they abstained from swimming and plunging themselves," [i.e., diving,] "they discoursed of many things relating to the Baths of the Ancients, and the Origine of Springs. When they had in this manner passed away an hour, they stepped out of the bath; and, having dried and cloathed themselves, they sate down in expectation of such a supper as the place afforded; designing to refresh themselves like the Deipnosophilæ, and rather to reason than to drink profoundly. But in this innocent intention they were interrupted by the disturbance arising from a little quarrel, in which some of the ruder people in the house were for a short time engaged. At this Mr. Hobbes seemed much concerned, though he was at some distance from the persons." And why was he concerned, gentlemen? No doubt you fancy, from, some benign and disinterested love of peace and harmony, worthy of an old man and a philosopher. But listen—"For a while he was not composed, but related it once or twice as to himself, with a low and careful tone, how Sextus

Roscius was murthered after supper by the Balneæ Palatinæ. Of such general extent is that remark of Cicero, in relation to Epicurus the Atheist, of whom he observed that he of all men dreaded most those things which he contemned—Death and the Gods." Merely because it was supper time, and in the neighborhood of a bath, Mr. Hobbes must have the fate of Sextus Roscius. What logic was there in this, unless to a man who was always dreaming of murder? Here was Leviathan, no longer afraid of the daggers of English cavaliers or French clergy, but "frightened from his propriety" by a row in an ale-house between some honest clod-hoppers of Derbyshire, whom his own gaunt scare-crow of a person that belonged to quite another century, would have frightened out of their wits.

Malebranche, it will give you pleasure to hear, was murdered. The man who murdered him is well known: it was Bishop Berkeley. The story is familiar, though hitherto not put in a proper light. Berkeley, when a young man, went to Paris and called on Père Malebranche. He found him in his cell cooking. Cooks have ever been a genus irritabile; authors still more so: Malebranche was both: a dispute arose; the old father, warm already, became warmer; culinary and metaphysical irritations united to derange his liver: he took to his bed, and died. Such is the common version of the story: "So the whole ear of Denmark is abused." The fact is, that the matter was hushed up, out of consideration for Berkeley, who (as Pope remarked) had "every virtue under heaven:" else it was well known that Berkeley, feeling himself nettled by the waspishness of the old Frenchman, squared at him; a turn-up was the consequence: Malebranche was floored in the first round; the conceit was wholly taken out of him; and he would perhaps have given in; but Berkeley's blood was now up, and he insisted on the old Frenchman's retracting his doctrine of Occasional Causes. The vanity of the man was too great for this; and he fell a sacrifice to the impetuosity of Irish youth, combined with his own absurd obstinacy.

Leibnitz, being every way superior to Malebranche, one might, a fortiori, have counted on his being murdered; which, however, was not the case. I believe he was nettled at this neglect, and felt himself insulted by the security in which he passed his days. In no other way can I explain his conduct at the latter end of his life, when he chose to grow very avaricious, and to hoard up large sums of gold, which he kept in his own house. This was at Vienna, where he died; and letters are still in existence, describing the immeasurable anxiety which he entertained for his throat. Still his ambition, for being attempted at least, was so great, that he would not forego the danger. A late English pedagogue, of Birmingham manufacture, viz., Dr. Parr, took a more selfish course, under the same circumstances. He had amassed a considerable quantity of gold and silver plate, which was for some time deposited in his bed-room at his parsonage house, Hatton. But growing every day more afraid of being murdered, which he knew that he could not stand, (and to which, indeed, he never had the slightest pretension,) he transferred the whole to the Hatton blacksmith; conceiving, no doubt, that the murder of a blacksmith would fall more lightly on the salus reipublicæ, than that of a pedagogue. But I have heard this greatly disputed; and it seems now generally agreed, that one good horse-shoe is worth about 2 1/4 Spital sermons.

As Leibnitz, though not murdered, may be said to have died, partly of the fear that he should be murdered, and partly of vexation that he was not,—Kant, on the other hand—who had no ambition in that way—had a narrower escape from a murderer than any man we read of, except Des Cartes. So absurdly does fortune throw about her favors! The case is told, I think, in an anonymous life of this very great man. For health's sake, Kant imposed upon himself, at one time, a walk of six miles every day along a highroad. This fact becoming known to a man who had his private reasons for committing murder, at the third milestone from Königsberg, he waited for his "intended," who came up to time as duly as a mailcoach. But for an accident, Kant was a dead man. However, on considerations of "morality," it happened that the murderer preferred a little child, whom he saw playing in the road, to the old transcendentalist: this child he murdered; and thus it happened that Kant escaped. Such is the German account of the matter; but my opinion is—that the murderer was an amateur, who felt how little would be gained to the cause of good taste by murdering an old, arid, and adust metaphysician; there was no room for display, as the man could not possibly look more like a mummy when dead, than he had done alive.

Thus, gentlemen, I have traced the connection between philosophy and our art, until insensibly I find that I have wandered into our own era. This I shall not take any pains to characterize apart from that which preceded it, for, in fact, they have no distinct character. The seventeenth and eighteenth centuries, together with so much of the nineteenth as we have yet seen, jointly compose the Augustan age of murder. The finest work of the seventeenth century is, unquestionably, the murder of Sir Edmondbury Godfrey, which has my entire approbation. At the same time, it must be observed, that the quantity of murder was not great in this century, at least amongst our own artists; which, perhaps, is attributable to the want of enlightened patronage. Sint Mæcenates, non deerunt, Flacce, Marones. Consulting Grant's "Observations on the Bills of Mortality," (4th edition, Oxford, 1665,) I find, that out of 229,250, who died in London during one period of twenty years in the seventeenth century, not more than eighty-six were murdered; that is, about four three-tenths per annum. A small number this, gentlemen, to found an academy upon; and certainly, where the quantity is so small, we have a right to expect that the quality should be first-rate. Perhaps it was; yet, still I am of opinion that the best artist in this century was not equal to the best in that which followed. For instance, however praiseworthy the case of Sir Edmondbury Godfrey may be (and nobody can be more sensible of its merits than I am), still I cannot consent to place it on a level with that of Mrs. Ruscombe of Bristol, either as to originality of design, or boldness and breadth of style. This good lady's murder took place early in the reign of George III., a reign which was notoriously favorable to the arts generally. She lived in College Green, with a single maid-servant, neither of them having any pretension to the notice of history but what they derived from the great artist whose workmanship I am recording. One fine morning, when all Bristol was alive and in motion, some suspicion arising, the neighbors forced an entrance into the house, and found Mrs. Ruscombe murdered in her bed-room, and the servant murdered on the stairs: this was at noon; and, not more than two hours before, both mistress and servant had been seen alive. To the best of my remembrance, this was in 1764; upwards of sixty years, therefore, have now elapsed, and yet the artist is still undiscovered. The suspicions of posterity have settled upon two pretenders—a baker and a chimney-sweeper. But posterity is wrong; no unpractised artist could have conceived so bold an idea as that of a noon-day murder in the heart of a great city. It was no obscure baker, gentlemen, or anonymous chimney-sweeper, be assured, that executed this work. I know who it was. (Here there was a general buzz, which at length broke out into open applause; upon which the lecturer blushed, and went on with much earnestness.) For Heaven's sake, gentlemen, do not mistake me; it was not I that did it. I have not the vanity to think myself equal to any such achievement; be assured that you greatly overrate my poor talents; Mrs. Ruscombe's affair was far beyond my slender abilities. But I came to know who the artist was, from a celebrated surgeon, who assisted at his dissection. This gentleman had a private museum in the way of his profession, one corner of which was occupied by a cast from a man of remarkably fine proportions.

"That," said the surgeon, "is a cast from the celebrated Lancashire highwayman, who concealed his profession for some time from his neighbors, by drawing woollen stockings over his horse's legs, and in that way muffling the clatter which he must else have made in riding up a flagged alley that led to his stable. At the time of his execution for highway robbery, I was studying under Cruickshank: and the man's figure was so uncommonly fine, that no money or exertion was spared to get into possession of him with the least possible delay. By the connivance of the under-sheriff he was cut down within the legal time, and instantly put into a chaise and four; so that, when he reached Cruickshank's he was positively not dead. Mr. ——, a young student at that time, had the honor of giving him the coup de grâce, and finishing the sentence of the law." This remarkable anecdote, which seemed to imply that all the gentlemen in the dissecting-room were amateurs of our class, struck me a good deal; and I was repeating it one day to a Lancashire lady, who thereupon informed me, that she had herself lived in the neighborhood of that highwayman, and well remembered two circumstances, which combined, in the opinion of all his neighbors, to fix upon him the credit of Mrs. Ruscombe's affair. One was, the fact of his absence for a whole fortnight at the period of that murder: the other, that, within a very little time after, the neighborhood of this highwayman was deluged with dollars: now Mrs. Ruscombe was known to have hoarded about two thousand of that coin. Be the artist, however, who he might, the affair remains a durable monument of his genius; for such was the impression of awe, and the sense of power left behind, by the strength of conception manifested in this murder, that no tenant (as I was told in 1810) had been found up to that time for Mrs. Ruscombe's house.

But, whilst I thus eulogize the Ruscombian case, let me not be supposed to overlook the many other specimens of extraordinary merit spread over the face of this century. Such cases, indeed, as that of Miss Bland, or of Captain Donnellan, and Sir Theophilus Boughton, shall never have any countenance from me. Fie on these dealers in poison, say I: can they not keep to the old honest way of cutting throats, without introducing such abominable innovations from Italy? I consider all these poisoning cases, compared with the legitimate style, as no better than wax-work by the side of sculpture, or a lithographic print by the side of a fine Volpato. But, dismissing these, there remain many excellent works of art in a pure style, such as nobody need be ashamed to own, as every candid connoisseur will admit. Candid, observe, I say; for great allowances must be made in these cases; no artist can ever be sure of carrying through his own fine preconception. Awkward disturbances will arise; people will not submit to have their throats cut quietly; they will run, they will kick, they will bite; and whilst the portrait painter often has to complain of too much torpor in his subject, the artist, in our line, is generally embarrassed by too much animation. At the same time, however disagreeable to the artist, this tendency in murder to excite and irritate the subject, is certainly one of its advantages to the world in general, which we ought not to overlook, since it favors the development of latent talent. Jeremy Taylor notices with admiration, the extraordinary leaps which people will take under the influence of fear. There was a striking instance of this in the recent case of the M'Keands; the boy cleared a height, such as he will never clear again to his dying day. Talents also of the most brilliant description for thumping, and indeed for all the gymnastic exercises, have sometimes been developed by the panic which accompanies our artists; talents else buried and hid under a bushel to the possessors, as much as to their friends. I remember an interesting illustration of this fact, in a case which I learned in Germany.

Riding one day in the neighborhood of Munich, I overtook a distinguished amateur of our society, whose name I shall conceal. This gentleman informed me that, finding himself wearied with the frigid pleasures (so he called them) of mere amateurship, he had quitted England for the continent—meaning to practise a little professionally. For this purpose he resorted to Germany, conceiving the police in that part of Europe to be more heavy and drowsy than elsewhere. His debut as a practitioner took place at Mannheim; and, knowing me to be a brother amateur, he freely communicated the whole of his maiden adventure. "Opposite to my lodging," said he, "lived a baker: he was somewhat of a miser, and lived quite alone. Whether it were his great expanse of chalky face, or what else, I know not—but the fact was, I 'fancied' him, and resolved to commence business upon his throat, which by the way he always carried bare—a fashion which is very irritating to my desires. Precisely at eight o'clock in the evening, I observed that he regularly shut up his windows. One night I watched him when thus engaged—bolted in after him—locked the door—and, addressing him with great suavity, acquainted him with the nature of my errand; at the same time advising him to make no resistance, which would be mutually unpleasant. So saying, I drew out my tools; and was proceeding to operate. But at this spectacle, the baker, who seemed to have been struck by catalepsy at my first announce, awoke into tremendous agitation. 'I will not be murdered!' he shrieked aloud; 'what for will I lose my precious throat?' 'What for?' said I; 'if for no other reason, for this—that you put alum into your bread. But no matter, alum or no alum, (for I was resolved to forestall any argument on that point,) know that I am a virtuoso in the art of murder—am desirous of improving myself in its details—and am enamored of your vast surface of throat, to which I am determined to be a customer.' 'Is it so?' said he, 'but I'll find you custom in another line;' and so saying, he threw himself into a boxing attitude. The very idea of his boxing struck me as ludicrous. It is true, a London baker had distinguished himself in the ring, and became known to fame under the title of the Master of the Rolls; but he was young and unspoiled: whereas this man was a monstrous feather-bed in person, fifty years old, and totally out of condition. Spite of all this, however, and contending against me, who am a master in the art, he made so desperate a defence, that many times I feared he might turn the tables upon me; and that I, an amateur, might be murdered by a rascally baker. What a situation! Minds of sensibility will sympathize with my anxiety. How severe it was, you may understand by this, that for the first thirteen rounds the baker had the advantage. Round the fourteenth, I received a blow on the right eye, which closed it up; in the end, I believe, this was my salvation: for the anger it roused in me was so great that, in this and every one of the three following rounds, I floored the baker.

"Round 18th. The baker came up piping, and manifestly the worse for wear. His geometrical exploits in the four last rounds had done him no good. However, he showed some skill in stopping a message which I was sending to his cadaverous mug; in delivering which, my foot slipped, and I went down. "Round 19th. Surveying the baker, I became ashamed of having been so much bothered by a shapeless mass of dough; and I went in fiercely, and administered some severe punishment. A rally took place—both went down—baker undermost—ten to three on amateur.

"Round 20th. The baker jumped up with surprising agility; indeed, he managed his pins capitally, and fought wonderfully, considering that he was drenched in perspiration; but the shine was now taken out of him, and his game was the mere effect of panic. It was now clear that he could not last much longer. In the course of this round we tried the weaving system, in which I had greatly the advantage, and hit him repeatedly on the conk. My reason for this was, that his conk was covered with carbuncles; and I thought I should vex him by taking such liberties with his conk, which in fact I did.

"The three next rounds, the master of the rolls staggered about like a cow on the ice. Seeing how matters stood, in round twenty-fourth I whispered something into his ear, which sent him down like a shot. It was nothing more than my private opinion of the value of his throat at an annuity office. This little confidential whisper affected him greatly; the very perspiration was frozen on his face, and for the next two rounds I had it all my own way. And when I called time for the twenty-seventh round, he lay like a log on the floor."

After which, said I to the amateur, "It may be

presumed that you accomplished your purpose." "You are right," said he mildly, "I did; and a great satisfaction, you know, it was to my mind, for by this means I killed two birds with one stone;" meaning that he had both thumped the baker and murdered him. Now, for the life of me, I could not see that; for, on the contrary, to my mind it appeared that he had taken two stones to kill one bird, having been obliged to take the conceit out of him first with his fist, and then with his tools. But no matter for his logic. The moral of his story was good, for it showed what an astonishing stimulus to latent talent is contained in any reasonable prospect of being murdered. A pursy, unwieldy, half cataleptic baker of Mannheim had absolutely fought six-and-twenty rounds with an accomplished English boxer merely upon this inspiration; so greatly was natural genius exalted and sublimed by the genial presence of his murderer.

Really, gentlemen, when one hears of such things as these, it becomes a duty, perhaps, a little to soften that extreme asperity with which most men speak of murder. To hear people talk, you would suppose that all the disadvantages and inconveniences were on the side of being murdered, and that there were none at all in not being murdered. But considerate men think otherwise. "Certainly," says Jeremy Taylor, "it is a less temporal evil to fall by the rudeness of a sword than the violence of a fever: and the axe" (to which he might have added the ship-carpenter's mallet and the crow-bar) "a much less affliction than a strangury." Very true; the bishop talks like a wise man and an amateur, as he is; and another great philosopher, Marcus Aurelius, was equally above the vulgar prejudices on this subject. He declares it to be one of "the noblest functions of reason to know whether it is time to walk out of the world or not." (Book III., Collers' Translation.) No sort of knowledge being rarer than this, surely that man must be a most philanthropic character, who undertakes to instruct people in this branch of knowledge gratis, and at no little hazard to himself. All this, however, I throw out only in the way of speculation to future moralists; declaring in the meantime my own private conviction, that very few men commit murder upon philanthropic or patriotic principles, and repeating what I have already said once at least—that, as to the majority of murderers, they are very incorrect characters.

With respect to Williams's murders, the sublimest and most entire in their excellence that ever were committed, I shall not allow myself to speak incidentally. Nothing less than an entire lecture, or even an entire course of lectures, would suffice to expound their merits. But one curious fact, connected with his case, I shall mention, because it seems to imply that the blaze of his genius absolutely dazzled the eye of criminal justice. You all remember, I doubt not, that the instruments with which he executed his first great work, (the murder of the Marrs,) were a ship-carpenter's mallet and a knife. Now the mallet belonged to an old Swede, one John Petersen, and bore his initials. This instrument Williams left behind him, in Marr's house, and it fell into the hands of the magistrates. Now, gentlemen, it is a fact that the publication of this circumstance of the initials led immediately to the apprehension of Williams, and, if made earlier, would have prevented his second great work, (the murder of the Williamsons,) which took place precisely twelve days after. But the magistrates kept back this fact from the public for the entire twelve days, and until that second work was accomplished. That finished, they published it, apparently feeling that Williams had now done enough for his fame, and that his glory was at length placed beyond the reach of accident.

As to Mr. Thurtell's case, I know not what to say. Naturally, I have every disposition to think highly of my predecessor in the chair of this society; and I acknowledge that his lectures were unexceptionable. But, speaking ingenuously, I do really think that his principal performance, as an artist, has been much overrated. I admit that at first I was myself carried away by the general enthusiasm. On the morning when the murder was made known in London, there was the fullest meeting of amateurs that I have ever known since the days of Williams; old bed-ridden connoisseurs, who had got into a peevish way of sneering and complaining "that there was nothing doing," now hobbled down to our club-room: such hilarity, such benign expression of general satisfaction, I have rarely witnessed. On every side you saw people shaking hands, congratulating each other, and forming dinner parties for the evening; and nothing was to be heard but triumphant challenges of—"Well! will this do?" "Is this the right thing?" "Are you satisfied at last?" But, in the midst of this, I remember we all grew silent on hearing the old cynical amateur, L. S——, that laudator temporis acti, stumping along with his wooden leg; he entered the room with his usual scowl, and, as he advanced, he continued to growl and stutter the whole way—"Not an original idea in the whole piece—mere plagiarism,—base plagiarism from hints that I threw out! Besides, his style is as hard as Albert Durer, and as coarse as Fuseli." Many thought that this was mere jealousy, and general waspishness; but I confess that, when the first glow of enthusiasm had subsided, I have found most judicious critics to agree that there was something falsetto in the style of Thurtell. The fact is, he was a member of our society, which naturally gave a friendly bias to our judgments; and his person was universally familiar to the cockneys, which gave him, with the whole London public, a temporary popularity, that his pretensions are not capable of supporting; for *opinionum commenta delet dies, naturæ judicia confirmat.* There was, however, an unfinished design of Thurtell's for the murder of a man with a pair of dumb-bells, which I admired greatly; it was a mere outline, that he never completed; but to my mind it seemed every way superior to his chief work. I remember that there was great regret expressed by some amateurs that this sketch should have been left in an unfinished state: but there I cannot agree with them; for the fragments and first bold outlines of original artists have often a felicity about them which is apt to vanish in the management of the details.

The case of the M'Keands I consider far beyond the vaunted performance of Thurtell,—indeed above all praise; and bearing that relation, in fact, to the immortal works of Williams, which the Æneid bears to the Iliad.

But it is now time that I should say a few words about the principles of murder, not with a view to regulate your practice, but your judgment: as to old women, and the mob of newspaper readers, they are pleased with anything, provided it is bloody enough. But the mind of sensibility requires something more. *First,* then, let us speak of the kind of person who is adapted to the purpose of the murderer; *secondly,* of the place where; *thirdly,* of the time when, and other little circumstances.

As to the person, I suppose it is evident that he ought to be a good man; because, if he were not, he might himself, by possibility, be contemplating murder at the very time; and such "diamond-cut-diamond" tussles, though pleasant enough where nothing better is stirring, are really not what a critic can allow himself to call murders. I could mention some people (I name no names) who have been murdered by other people in a dark lane; and so far all seemed correct enough; but, on looking farther into the matter, the public have become aware that the murdered party was himself, at the moment, planning to rob his murderer, at the least, and possibly to murder him, if he had been strong enough. Whenever that is the case, or may be thought to be the case, farewell to all the genuine effects of the art. For the final purpose of murder, considered as a fine art, is precisely the same as that of tragedy, in Aristotle's account of it, viz., "to cleanse the heart by means of pity and terror." Now, terror there may be, but how can there be any pity for one tiger destroyed by another tiger?

It is also evident that the person selected ought not to be a public character. For instance, no judicious artist would have attempted to murder Abraham Newland. For the case was this; everybody read so much about Abraham Newland, and so few people ever saw him, that there was a fixed belief that he was an abstract idea. And I remember that once, when I happened to mention that I had dined at a coffee-house in company with Abraham Newland, everybody looked scornfully at me, as though I had pretended to have played at billiards with Prester John, or to have had an affair of honor with the Pope. And, by the way, the Pope would be a very improper person to murder: for he has such a virtual ubiquity as the father of Christendom, and, like the cuckoo, is so often heard but never seen, that I suspect most people regard *him* also as an abstract idea. Where, indeed, a public character is in the habit of giving dinners, "with every delicacy of the season," the case is very different: every person is satisfied that *he* is no abstract idea; and, therefore, there can be no impropriety in murdering him; only that his murder will fall into the class of assassinations, which I have not yet treated.

Thirdly. The subject chosen ought to be in good health: for it is absolutely barbarous to murder a sick person, who is usually quite unable to bear it. On this principle, no cockney ought to be chosen who is above twenty-five, for after that age he is sure to be dyspeptic. Or at least, if a man will hunt in that warren, he ought to murder a couple at one time; if the cockneys chosen should be tailors, he will of course think it his duty, on the old established equation, to murder eighteen. And, here, in this attention to the comfort of sick people, you will observe the usual effect of a fine art to soften and refine the feelings. The world in general, gentlemen, are very bloody-minded; and all they want in a murder is a copious effusion of blood; gaudy display in this point is enough for *them*. But the enlightened connoisseur is more refined in his taste; and from our art, as from all the other liberal arts when thoroughly cultivated, the result is—to improve and to humanize the heart; so true is it, that—

> "Ingenuas didicisse fideliter
>   artes,
> Emollit mores, nec sinit esse
>   feros."

A philosophic friend, well known for his philanthropy and general benignity, suggests that the subject chosen ought also to have a family of young children wholly dependent on his exertions, by way of deepening the pathos. And, undoubtedly, this is a judicious caution. Yet I would not insist too keenly on this condition. Severe good taste unquestionably demands it; but still, where the man was otherwise unobjectionable in point of morals and health, I would not look with too curious a jealousy to a restriction which might have the effect of narrowing the artist's sphere.

So much for the person. As to the time, the place, and the tools, I have many things to say, which at present I have no room for. The good sense of the practitioner has usually directed him to night and privacy. Yet there have not been wanting cases where this rule was departed from with excellent effect. In respect to time, Mrs. Ruscombe's case is a beautiful exception, which I have already noticed; and in respect both to time and place, there is a fine exception in the annals of Edinburgh, (year 1805,) familiar to every child in Edinburgh, but which has unaccountably been defrauded of its due portion of fame amongst English amateurs. The case I mean is that of a porter to one of the banks, who was murdered whilst carrying a bag of money, in broad daylight, on turning out of the High Street, one of the most public streets in Europe, and the murderer is to this hour undiscovered.

> "Sed fugit interea, fugit ir-
> reparabile tcmpus,
> Singula dum capti circumvec-
> tamur amore."

And now, gentlemen, in conclusion, let me again solemnly disclaim all pretensions on my own part to the character of a professional man. I never attempted any murder in my life, except in the year 1801, upon the body of a tom-cat; and that turned out differently from my intention. My purpose, I own, was downright murder. "Semper ego auditor tantum?" said I, "nunquamne reponam?" And I went down stairs in search of Tom at one o'clock on a dark night, with the "animus," and no doubt with the fiendish looks, of a murderer. But when I found him, he was in the act of plundering the pantry of bread and other things. Now this gave a new turn to the affair; for the time being one of general scarcity, when even Christians were reduced to the use of potato-bread, rice-bread, and all sorts of things, it was downright treason in a tom-cat to be wasting good wheaten-bread in the way he was doing. It instantly became a patriotic duty to put him to death; and as I raised aloft and shook the glittering steel, I fancied myself rising like Brutus, effulgent from a crowd of patriots, and, as I stabbed him, I

> "called aloud on Tully's name,
>   And bade the father of his
>   country hail!"

Since then, what wandering thoughts I may have had of attempting the life of an ancient ewe, of a superannuated hen, and such "small deer," are locked up in the secrets of my own breast; but for the higher departments of the art, I confess myself to be utterly unfit. My ambition does not rise so high. No, gentlemen, in the words of Horace,

> "——fungos vice cotis, ex-

> cutum Reddere ere quæ
> ferrum valet, exsors ipsa
> secandi."

---

1. Kant—who carried his demands of unconditional veracity to so extravagant a length as to affirm, that, if a man were to see an innocent person escape from a murderer, it would be his duty, on being questioned by the murderer, to tell the truth, and to point out the retreat of the innocent person, under any certainty of causing murder. Lest this doctrine should be supposed to have escaped him in any heat of dispute, on being taxed with it by a celebrated French writer, he solemnly reaffirmed it, with his reasons.
2. "June 1, 1675.—Drinke part of 3 boules of punch, (a liquor very strainge to me,)" says the Rev. Mr. Henry Teonge, in his Diary lately published. In a note on this passage, a reference is made to Fryer's Travels to the East Indies, 1672, who speaks of "that enervating liquor called Paunch, (which is Indostan for five,) from five ingredients." Made thus, it seems the medical men called it Diapente; if with four only, Diatessaron. No doubt, it was its Evangelical name that recommended it to the Rev. Mr. Teonge.

SECOND PAPER ON MURDER, CONSIDERED AS ONE OF THE FINE ARTS.

(1839)

Doctor North: You are a liberal man: liberal in the true classical sense, not in the slang sense of modern politicians and education-mongers. Being so, I am sure that you will sympathize with my case. I am an ill-used man, Dr. North—particularly ill used; and, with your permission, I will briefly explain how. A black scene of calumny will be laid open; but you, Doctor, will make all things square again. One frown from you, directed to the proper quarter, or a warning shake of the crutch, will set me right in public opinion, which at present, I am sorry to say, is rather hostile to me and mine—all owing to the wicked arts of slanderers. But you shall hear.

A good many years ago you may remember

that I came forward in the character of a *dilettante* in murder. Perhaps *dilettante* may be too strong a word. *Connoisseur* is better suited to the scruples and infirmity of public taste. I suppose there is no harm in *that* at least. A man is not bound to put his eyes, ears, and understanding into his breeches pocket when he meets with a murder. If he is not in a downright comatose state, I suppose he must see that one murder is better or worse than another in point of good taste. Murders have their little differences and shades of merit as well as statues, pictures, oratorios, cameos, intaglios, or what not. You may be angry with the man for talking too much, or too publicly, (as to the too much, that I deny—a man can never cultivate his taste too highly;) but you must allow him to think, at any rate; and you, Doctor, you think, I am sure, both deeply and correctly on the subject. Well, would you believe it? all my neighbors came to hear of that little æsthetic essay which you had published; and, unfortunately, hearing at the very same time of a club that I as connected with, and a dinner at which I presided—both tending to the same little object as the essay, viz., the diffusion of a just taste among her majesty's subjects, they got up the most barbarous calumnies against me. In particular, they said that I, or that the club, which comes to the same thing, had offered bounties on well conducted homicides—with a scale of draw-backs, in case of any one defect or flaw, according to a table issued to private friends. Now, Doctor, I'll tell you the whole truth about the dinner and the club, and you'll see how malicious the world is. But first let me tell you, confidentially, what my real principles are upon the matters in question.

As to murder, I never committed one in my life. It's a well known thing amongst all my friends. I can get a paper to certify as much, signed by lots of people. Indeed, if you come to that, I doubt whether many people could produce as strong a certificate. Mine would be as big as a table-cloth. There is indeed one member of the club, who pretends to say that he caught me once making too free with his throat on a club night, after every body else had retired. But, observe, he shuffles in his story according to his state of civilation. When not far gone, he contents himself with saying that he caught me ogling his throat; and that I was melancholy for some weeks after, and that my voice sounded in a way expressing, to the nice ear of a connoisseur, *the sense of opportunities lost*—but the club all know that he's a disappointed man himself, and that he speaks querulously at times about the fatal neglect of a man's coming abroad without his tools. Besides, all this is an affair between two amateurs, and every body makes allowances for little asperities and sorenesses in such a case. "But," say you, "If no murderer, my correspondent may have encouraged, or even have bespoke a murder." No, upon

my honor—nothing of the kind. And that was the
very point I wished to argue for your satisfaction.
The truth is, I am a very particular man in everything relating to murder; and perhaps I carry my
delicacy too far. The Stagyrite most justly, and
possibly with a view to my case, placed virtue in
the [Greek: to meson] or middle point between
two extremes. A golden mean is certainly what
every man should aim at. But it is easier talking
than doing; and, my infirmity being notoriously
too much milkiness of heart, I find it difficult to
maintain that steady equatorial line between the
two poles of too much murder on the one hand,
and too little on the other. I am too soft—Doctor,
too soft; and people get excused through me—
nay, go through life without an attempt made
upon them, that ought not to be excused. I believe
if I had the management of things, there would
hardly be a murder from year's end to year's end.
In fact I'm for virtue, and goodness, and all that
sort of thing. And two instances I'll give you to
what an extremity I carry my virtue. The first may
seem a trifle; but not if you knew my nephew,
who was certainly born to be hanged, and would
have been so long ago, but for my restraining
voice. He is horribly ambitious, and thinks himself a man of cultivated taste in most branches of
murder, whereas, in fact, he has not one idea on
the subject, but such as he has stolen from me.
This is so well known, that the club has twice

blackballed him, though every indulgence was shown to him as my relative. People came to me and said—"Now really, President, we would do much to serve a relative of yours. But still, what can be said? You know yourself that he'll disgrace us. If we were to elect him, why, the next thing we should hear of would be some vile butcherly murder, by way of justifying our choice. And what sort of a concern would it be? You know, as well as we do, that it would be a disgraceful affair, more worthy of the shambles than of an artist's *attelier*. He would fall upon some great big man, some huge farmer returning drunk from a fair. There would be plenty of blood, and *that* he would expect us to take in lieu of taste, finish, scenical grouping. Then, again, how would he tool? Why, most probably with a cleaver and a couple of paving stones: so that the whole *coup d'oeil* would remind you rather of some hideous ogre or cyclops, than of the delicate operator of the nineteenth century." The picture was drawn with the hand of truth; *that* I could not but allow, and, as to personal feelings in the matter, I dismissed them from the first. The next morning I spoke to my nephew—I was delicately situated, as you see, but I determined that no consideration should induce me to flinch from my duty. "John," said I, "you seem to me to have taken an erroneous view of life and its duties. Pushed on by ambition, you are dreaming rather of what it might be glorious to attempt, than what it would be possible for you to accomplish. Believe me, it is not necessary to a man's respectability that he should commit a murder. Many a man has passed through life most respectably, without attempting any species of homicide—good, bad, or indifferent. It is your first duty to ask yourself, *quid valeant humeri, quid ferre recusent*? we cannot all be brilliant men in this life. And it is for your interest to be contented rather with a humble station well filled, than to shock every body with failures, the more conspicuous by contrast with the ostentation of their promises." John made no answer, he looked very sulky at the moment, and I am in high hopes that I have saved a near relation from making a fool of himself by attempting what is as much beyond his capacity as an epic poem. Others, however, tell me that he is meditating a revenge upon me and the whole club. But let this be as it may, *liberavi animam meam*; and, as you see, have run some risk with a wish to diminish the amount of homicide. But the other case still more forcibly illustrates my virtue. A man came to me as a candidate for the place of my servant, just then vacant. He had the reputation of having dabbled a little in our art; some said not without merit. What startled me, however, was, that he supposed this art to be part of his regular duties in my service. Now that was a thing I would not allow; so I said at once, "Richard (or James, as the case might be,) you misunderstand my character. If a man will and must practise this difficult (and allow me to add, dangerous) branch of art—if he has an overruling genius for it, why, he might as well pursue his studies whilst living in my service as in another's. And also, I may observe, that it can do no harm either to himself or to the subject on whom he operates, that he should be guided by men of more taste than himself. Genius may do much, but long study of the art must always entitle a man to offer advice. So far I will go—general principles I will suggest. But as to any particular case, once for all I will have nothing to do with it. Never tell me of any special work of art you are meditating—I set my face against it *in toto*. For if once a man indulges himself in murder, very soon he comes to think little of robbing; and from robbing he comes next to drinking and Sabbath-breaking, and from that to incivility and procrastination. Once begin upon this downward path, you never know where you are to stop. Many a man has dated his ruin from some murder or other that perhaps he thought little of at the time. *Principiis obsta*—that's my rule." Such was my speech, and I have always acted up to it; so if that is not being virtuous, I should be glad to know what is. But now about the dinner and the club. The club was not particularly of my creation; it arose pretty much as other similar associations, for the propagation of truth and the communication of new ideas, rather from the necessities of things than upon any one man's suggestion. As to the dinner, if any man more than another could be held responsible for that, it was a member known amongst us by the name of *Toad-in-the-hole*. He was so called from his gloomy misanthropical disposition, which led him into constant disparagements of all modern murders as vicious abortions, belonging to no authentic school of art. The finest performances of our own age he snarled at cynically; and at length this querulous humor grew upon him so much, and he became so notorious as a *laudator tentporis acti*, that few people cared to seek his society. This made him still more fierce and truculent. He went about muttering and growling; wherever you met him he was soliloquizing and saying, "despicable pretender—without grouping—without two ideas upon handling—without"—and there you lost him. At length existence seemed to be painful to him; he rarely spoke, he seemed conversing with phantoms in the air, his housekeeper informed us that his reading was nearly confined to God's Revenge upon Murder, by Reynolds, and a more ancient book of the same title, noticed by Sir Walter Scott in his *Fortunes of Nigel*. Sometimes, perhaps, he might read in the Newgate Calendar down to the year 1788, but he never looked into a book more recent. In fact, he had a theory with regard to the French Revolution, as having been the great cause of degeneration in murder. "Very soon, sir," he used to say, "men will have lost the art of killing poultry: the very rudiments of the art will have perished!" In the year 1811 he retired from general society. Toad-in-the-hole was no more seen in any public resort. We missed him from his wonted haunts—nor up the lawn, nor at the wood was he. By the side of the main conduit his listless length at noontide he would stretch, and pore upon the filth that muddled by. "Even dogs are not what they were, sir—not what they should be. I remember in my grandfather's time that some dogs had an idea of murder. I have known a mastiff lie in ambush for a rival, sir, and murder him with pleasing circumstances of good taste. Yes, sir, I knew a tom-cat that was an assassin. But now"— and then, the subject growing too painful, he dashed his hand to his forehead, and went off abruptly in a homeward direction towards his favorite conduit, where he was seen by an amateur in such a state that he thought it dangerous to address him. Soon after he shut himself entirely up; it was understood that he had resigned himself to melancholy; and at length the prevailing notion was, that Toad-in-the-hole had hanged himself.

The world was wrong *there*, as it has been on some other questions. Toad-in-the-hole might be sleeping, but dead he was not; and of that we soon had ocular proof. One morning in 1812, an amateur surprised us with the news that he had seen Toad-in-the-hole brushing with hasty steps the dews away to meet the postman by the conduit side. Even that was something: how much more, to hear that he had shaved his beard—had laid aside his sad-colored clothes, and was adorned like a bridegroom of ancient days. What could be the meaning of all this? Was Toad-in-the-hole mad? or how? Soon after the secret was explained—in more than a figurative sense "the murder was out." For in came the London morning papers, by which it appeared that but three days before a murder, the most superb of the century by many degrees had occurred in the heart of London. I need hardly say, that this was the great exterminating *chef-d'oeuvre* of Williams at Mr. Marr's, No. 29, Ratcliffe Highway. That was the *début* of the artist; at least for anything the public knew. What occurred at Mr. Williamson's twelve nights afterwards—the second work turned out from the same chisel—some people pronounced even superior. But Toad-in-the-hole always "reclaimed"—he was even angry at comparisons. "This vulgar *gout de comparaison*, as La Bruyère calls it," he would often remark, "will be our ruin; each work has its own separate characteristics—each in and for itself is incomparable. One, perhaps, might suggest the *Iliad*—the other the *Odyssey*: what do you get by such comparisons? Neither ever was, or will be surpassed; and when you've talked for hours, you must still come back to that." Vain, however, as all criticism might be, he often said that volumes might be written on each case for itself; and he even proposed to publish in quarto on the subject.

Meantime, how had Toad-in-the-hole happened to hear of this great work of art so early in the morning? He had received an account by express, dispatched by a correspondent in London, who watched the progress of art *On Toady's* behalf, with a general commission to send off a special express, at whatever cost, in the event of any estimable works appearing—how much more upon occasion of a *ne plus ultra* in art! The express arrived in the night-time; Toad-in-the-hole was then gone to bed; he had been muttering and grumbling for hours, but of course he was called up. On reading the account, he threw his arms round the express, called him his brother and his preserver; settled a pension upon him for three lives, and expressed his regret at not having it in his power to knight him. We, on our part—we amateurs, I mean—having heard that he was abroad, and therefore had *not* hanged himself, made sure of soon seeing him amongst us. Accordingly he soon arrived, knocked over the porter on his road to the reading-room; he seized every man's hand as he passed him—wrung it almost frantically, and kept ejaculating, "Why, now here's something like a murder!—this is the real thing—this is genuine—this is what you can approve, can recommend to a friend:

this—says every man, on reflection—this is the thing that ought to be!" Then, looking at particular friends, he said—"Why, Jack, how are you? Why, Tom, how are you? Bless me, you look ten years younger than when I last saw you." "No, sir," I replied, "It is you who look ten years younger." "Do I? well, I should'nt wonder if I did; such works are enough to make us all young." And in fact the general opinion is, that Toad-in-the-hole would have died but for this regeneration of art, which he called a second age of Leo the Tenth; and it was our duty, he said solemnly, to commemorate it. At present, and *en attendant*—rather as an occasion for a public participation in public sympathy, than as in itself any commensurate testimony of our interest—he proposed that the club should meet and dine together. A splendid public dinner, therefore, was given by the club; to which all amateurs were invited from a distance of one hundred miles.

Of this dinner there are ample short-hand notes amongst the archives of the club. But they are not "extended," to speak diplomatically; and the reporter is missing—I believe, murdered. Meantime, in years long after that day, and on an occasion perhaps equally interesting, viz., the turning up of Thugs and Thuggism, another dinner was given. Of this I myself kept notes, for fear of another accident to the short-hand reporter. And I here subjoin them. Toad-in-the-hole, I must mention, was present at this dinner. In fact, it was one of its sentimental incidents. Being as old as the valleys at the dinner of 1812, naturally he was as old as the hills at the Thug dinner of 1838. He had taken to wearing his beard again; why, or with what view, it passes my persimmon to tell you. But so it was. And his appearance was most benign and venerable. Nothing could equal the angelic radiance of his smile as he inquired after the unfortunate reporter, (whom, as a piece of private scandal, I should tell you that he was himself supposed to have murdered, in a rapture of creative art:) the answer was, with roars of laughter, from the under-sheriff of our county—"Non est inventus." Toad-in-the-hole laughed outrageously at this: in fact, we all thought he was choking; and, at the earnest request of the company, a musical composer furnished a most beautiful glee upon the occasion, which was sung five times after dinner, with universal applause and inextinguishable laughter, the words being these, (and the chorus so contrived, as most beautifully to mimic the peculiar laughter of Toad-in-the-hole:)

—

> "Et interrogatum est à Toad-
> in-the hole—Ubi est ille
> reporter?
> Et responsum est cum

cachinno—Non est
inventus."
CHORUS.
"Deinde iteratum est ab omnibus, cum cachinnatione
undulante—
Non est inventus."

Toad-in-the-hole, I ought to mention, about nine years before, when an express from Edinburgh brought him the earliest intelligence of the Burke-and-Hare revolution in the art, went mad upon the spot; and, instead of a pension to the express for even one life, or a knighthood, endeavored to burke him; in consequence of which he was put into a strait waistcoat. And that was the reason we had no dinner then. But now all of us were alive and kicking, strait-waistcoaters and others; in fact, not one absentee was reported upon the entire roll. There were also many foreign amateurs present.

Dinner being over, and the cloth drawn, there was a general call made for the new glee of *Non est inventus*; but, as this would have interfered with the requisite gravity of the company during the earlier toasts, I overruled the call. After the national toasts had been given, the first official toast of the day was, *The Old Man of the Mountains*—drunk in solemn silence.

Toad-in-the-hole returned thanks in a neat

speech. He likened himself to the Old Man of the Mountains, in a few brief allusions, that made the company absolutely yell with laughter; and he concluded with giving the health of

Mr. Von Hammer, with many thanks to him for his learned History of the Old Man and his subjects the assassins.

Upon this I rose and said, that doubtless most of the company were aware of the distinguished place assigned by orientalists to the very learned Turkish scholar Von Hammer the Austrian; that he had made the profoundest researches into our art as connected with those early and eminent artists the Syrian assassins in the period of the Crusaders; that his work had been for several years deposited, as a rare treasure of art, in the library of the club. Even the author's name, gentlemen, pointed him out as the historian of our art—Von Hammer—

"Yes, yes," interrupted Toad-in-the-hole, who never can sit still—"Yes, yes, Von Hammer—he's the man for a *malleus hæreticorum*: think rightly of our art, or he's the man to tickle your catastrophes. You all know what consideration Williams bestowed on the hammer, or the ship carpenter's mallet, which is the same thing. Gentlemen, I give you another great hammer—Charles the Hammer, the Marteau, or, in old French, the Martel—he hammered the Saracens till they were all as dead as door-nails—he did, believe me."

"*Charles Martel,* with all the honors."

But the explosion of Toad-in-the-hole, together with the uproarious cheers for the grandpapa of Charlemagne, had now made the company unmanageable. The orchestra was again challenged with shouts the stormiest for the new glee. I made again a powerful effort to overrule the challenge. I might as well have talked to the winds. I foresaw a tempestuous evening; and I ordered myself to be strengthened with three waiters on each side; the vice-president with as many. Symptoms of unruly enthusiasm were beginning to show out; and I own that I myself was considerably excited as the orchestra opened with its storm of music, and the impassioned glee began—"*Et interrogatum est à Toad-in-the-hole—Ubi est ille Reporter?*" And the frenzy of the passion became absolutely convulsing, as the full chorus fell in—"*Et iteratum est ab omnibus—Non est inventus*"

By this time I saw how things were going: wine and music were making most of the amateurs wild. Particularly Toad-in-the-hole, though considerably above a hundred years old, was getting as vicious as a young leopard. It was a fixed impression with the company that he had murdered the reporter in the year 1812; since which time (viz. twenty-six years) "ille reporter" had been constantly reported "Non est inventus." Consequently, the glee about himself, which of itself was most tumultuous and jubilant, carried him off his feet. Like the famous choral songs amongst the citizens of Abdera, nobody could hear it without a contagious desire for falling back into the agitating music of "Et interrogatum est à Toad-in-the-hole," &c. I enjoined vigilance upon my assessors, and the business of the evening proceeded.

The next toast was—*The Jewish Sicarii.*

Upon which I made the following explanation to the company:—"Gentlemen, I am sure it will interest you all to hear that the assassins, ancient as they were, had a race of predecessors in the very same country. All over Syria, but particularly in Palestine, during the early years of the Emperor Nero, there was a band of murderers, who prosecuted their studies in a very novel manner. They did not practise in the night-time, or in lonely places; but justly considering that great crowds are in themselves a sort of darkness by means of the dense pressure and the impossibility of finding out who it was that gave the blow, they mingled with mobs everywhere; particularly at the great paschal feast in Jerusalem; where they actually had the audacity, as Josephus assures us, to press into the temple,—and whom should they choose for operating upon but Jonathan himself, the Pontifex Maximus? They murdered him, gentlemen, as beautifully as if they had had him alone on a moonless night in a dark lane. And when it was asked, who was the murderer, and where he was"—

"Why, then, it was answered," interrupted Toad-in-the-hole, "*Non est inventus*." And then, in spite of all I could do or say, the orchestra opened, and the whole company began—"Et interrogatum est à Toad-in-the-hole—Ubi est ille Sicarius? Et responsum est ab omnibus—*Non est inventus*."

When the tempestuous chorus had subsided, I began again:—"Gentlemen, you will find a very circumstantial account of the Sicarii in at least three different parts of Josephus; once in Book XX. sect. v. c. 8, of his *Antiquities*; once in Book I. of his *Wars*: but in sect. 10 of the chapter first cited you will find a particular description of their tooling. This is what he says—'They tooled with small scymetars not much different from the Persian *acinacæ*, but more curved, and for all the world most like the Roman sickles or *sicæ*.' It is perfectly magnificent, gentlemen, to hear the sequel of their history. Perhaps the only case on record where a regular army of murderers was assembled, a *justus exercitus*, was in the case of these *Sicarii*. They mustered in such strength in the wilderness, that Festus himself was obliged to march against them with the Roman legionary force."

Upon which Toad-in-the-hole, that cursed interrupter, broke out a-singing—"Et interrogatum est à Toad-in-the-hole—Ubi est ille exercitus? Et responsum est ab omnibus—Non est inventus."

"No, no, Toad—you are wrong for once: that army *was* found, and was all cut to pieces in the desert. Heavens, gentlemen, what a sublime picture! The Roman legions—the wilderness—Jerusalem in the distance—an army of murderers in the foreground!"

Mr. R., a member, now gave the next toast—"To the further improvement of Tooling, and thanks to the Committee for their services."

Mr. L., on behalf of the committee who had reported on that subject, returned thanks. He made an interesting extract from the report, by which it appeared how very much stress had been laid formerly on the mode of tooling, by the fathers, both Greek and Latin. In confirmation of this pleasing fact, he made a very striking statement in reference to the earliest work of antediluvian art. Father Mersenne, that learned Roman Catholic, in page one thousand four hundred and thirty-one [1] of his operose Commentary on Genesis, mentions, on the authority of several rabbis, that the quarrel of Cain with Abel was about a young woman; that, by various accounts, Cain had tooled with his teeth, [Abelem fuisse *morsibus* dilaceratum à Cain;] by many others, with the jaw-bone of an ass; which is the tooling adopted by most painters. But it is pleasing to the mind of sensibility to know that, as science expanded, sounder views were adopted. One author contends for a pitchfork, St. Chrysostom for a sword, Irenæus for a scythe, and Prudentius for a hedging-bill. This last writer delivers his opinion thus:—

"Frater, probatæ sanctitatis
æmulus,
Germana curvo colla frangit
sarculo:"

i.e. his brother, jealous of his attested sanctity, fractures his brotherly throat with a curved hedging-bill. "All which is respectfully submitted by your committee, not so much as decisive of the question, (for it is not,) but in order to impress upon the youthful mind the importance which has ever been attached to the quality of the tooling by such men as Chrysostom and Irenæus."

"Dang Irenæus!" said Toad-in-the-hole, who now rose impatiently to give the next toast:—"Our Irish friends; and a speedy revolution in their mode of tooling, as well as everything else connected with the art!"

"Gentlemen, I'll tell you the plain truth. Every day of the year we take up a paper, we read the opening of a murder. We say, this is good, this is charming, this is excellent! But, behold you! scarcely have we read a little farther, before the word Tipperary or Ballina-something betrays the Irish manufacture. Instantly we loath it; we call to the waiter; we say, Waiter, take away this paper; send it out of the house; it is absolutely offensive to all just taste.' I appeal to every man whether, on finding a murder (otherwise perhaps promising enough) to be Irish, he does not feel himself as much insulted as when Madeira being ordered, he finds it to be Cape; or when, taking up what he takes to be a mushroom, it turns out what children call a toad-stool. Tithes, politics, or something wrong in principle, vitiate every Irish murder. Gentlemen, this must be reformed, or Ireland will not be a land to live in; at least, if we do live there, we must import all our murders, that's clear." Toad-in-the-hole sat down growling with suppressed wrath, and the universal "Hear, hear!" sufficiently showed that he spoke the general feeling.

The next toast was—"The sublime epoch of Burkism and Harism!"

This was drunk with enthusiasm; and one of the members, who spoke to the question, made a very curious communication to the company: —"Gentlemen, we fancy Burkism to be a pure invention of our own times: and in fact no Pancirollus has ever enumerated this branch of art when writing *de rebus deperditis*. Still I have ascertained that the essential principle of the art *was* known to the ancients, although like the art of painting upon glass, of making the myrrhine cups, &c., it was lost in the dark ages for want of encouragement. In the famous collection of Greek epigrams made by Planudes is one upon a very charming little case of Burkism: it is a perfect little gem of art. The epigram itself I cannot lay my hand upon at this moment, but the following is an abstract of it by Salmasius, as I find it in his notes on Vopiscus: 'Est et elegans epigramma Lucilii, (well he might call it "elegans!") ubi medicus et pollinctor de compacto sic egerunt, ut medicus ægros omnes curæ suæ commissos occideret:' this was the basis of the contract, you see, that on the one part the doctor, for himself and his assigns, doth undertake and contract duly and truly to murder all the patients committed to his charge: but why? There lies the beauty of the case—'Et ut pollinctori amico suo traderet pollingendos.' The *pollinctor*, you are aware, was a person whose business it was to dress and prepare dead bodies for burial. The original ground of the transaction appears to have been sentimental: 'He was my friend,' says the murderous doctor; 'he was dear to me,' in speaking of the pollinctor. But the law, gentlemen, is stern and harsh: the law will not hear of these tender motives: to sustain a contract of this nature in law, it is essential that a 'consideration' should be given. Now what was the consideration? For thus far all is on the side of the pollinctor: he will be well paid for his services; but, meantime, the generous, the noble-minded doctor gets nothing. What was the little consideration again, I ask, which the law would insist on the doctor's taking? You shall hear: 'Et ut pollinctor vicissim [Greek: telamonas] quos furabatur de pollinctione mortuorum medico mitteret doni ad alliganda vulnera eorurn quos curabat.'

Now, the case is clear: the whole went on a principle of reciprocity which would have kept up the trade for ever. The doctor was also a surgeon: he could not murder *all* his patients: some of the surgical patients must be retained intact; *re infectâ.* For these he wanted linen bandages. But, unhappily, the Romans wore woollen, on which account they bathed so often. Meantime, there *was* linen to be had in Rome; but it was monstrously dear; and the [Greek: telamones] or linen swathing bandages, in which superstition obliged them to bind up corpses, would answer capitally for the surgeon. The doctor, therefore, contracts to furnish his friend with a constant succession of corpses, provided, and be it understood always, that his said friend in return should supply him with one half of the articles he would receive from the friends of the parties murdered or to be murdered. The doctor invariably recommended his invaluable friend the pollinctor, (whom let us call the undertaker;) the undertaker, with equal regard to the sacred rights of friendship, uniformly recommended the doctor. Like Pylades and Orestes, they were models of a perfect friendship: in their lives they were lovely, and on the gallows, it is to be hoped, they were not divided.

"Gentlemen, it makes me laugh horribly, when I think of those two friends drawing and redrawing on each other: 'Pollinctor in account with Doctor, debtor by sixteen corpses; creditor by forty-five bandages, two of which damaged.' Their names unfortunately are lost; but I conceive they must have been Quintus Burkius and Publius Harius. By the way, gentlemen, has anybody heard lately of Hare? I understand he is comfortably settled in Ireland, considerably to the west, and does a little business now and then; but, as he observes with a sigh, only as a retailer—nothing like the fine thriving wholesale concern so carelessly blown up at Edinburgh. 'You see what comes of neglecting business,'—is the chief moral, the [Greek: epimutheon], as Æsop would say, which he draws from his past experience."

At length came the toast of the day—*Thugdom in all its branches.*

The speeches *attempted* at this crisis of the dinner were past all counting. But the applause was so furious, the music so stormy, and the crashing of glasses so incessant, from the general resolution never again to drink an inferior toast from the same glass, that my power is not equal to the task of reporting. Besides which, Toad-in-the-hole now became quite ungovernable. He kept firing pistols in every direction; sent his servant for a blunderbuss, and talked of loading with ball-cartridge. We conceived that his former madness had returned at the mention of Burke and Hare; or that, being again weary of life, he had resolved to go off in a general massacre. This we could not think of allowing: it became indispensable, therefore, to kick him out, which we did with universal consent, the whole company lending their toes uno pede, as I may say, though pitying his gray hairs and his angelic smile. During the operation the orchestra poured in their old chorus. The universal company sang, and (what surprised us most of all) Toad-in-the-hole joined us furiously in singing—

> "Et interrogatum est ab om-
> nibus—Ubi est ille Toad-
> in-the-hole
> Et responsum est ab omnibus
> —Non est inventus."

---

1. "Page one thousand four hundred and thirty-one"—*literally*, good reader, and no joke at all.

THREE MEMORABLE MURDERS.

A SEQUEL TO 'MURDER CONSIDERED AS ONE OF THE FINE ARTS.

(1854)

It is impossible to conciliate readers of so saturnine and gloomy a class, that they cannot enter with genial sympathy into any gaiety whatever, but, least of all, when the gaiety trespasses a little into the province of the extravagant. In such a case, not to sympathize is not to understand; and the playfulness, which is not relished, becomes flat and insipid, or absolutely without meaning. Fortunately, after all such churls have withdrawn from my audience in high displeasure, there remains a large majority who are loud in acknowledging the amusement which they have derived from a former paper of mine, 'On Murder considered as one of the Fine Arts;' at the same time proving the sincerity of their praise by one

hesitating expression of censure. Repeatedly they
have suggested to me, that perhaps the extravagance, though clearly intentional, and forming
one element in the general gaiety of the conception, went too far. I am not myself of that opinion;
and I beg to remind these friendly censors, that it
is amongst the direct purposes and efforts of this
bagatelle to graze the brink of horror, and of all
that would in actual realization be most repulsive.
The very excess of the extravagance, in fact, by
suggesting to the reader continually the mere aeri-
ality of the entire speculation, furnishes the surest
means of disenchanting him from the horror
which might else gather upon his feelings. Let me
remind such objectors, once for all, of Dean Swift's
proposal for turning to account the supernu-
merary infants of the three kingdoms, which, in
those days, both at Dublin and at London, were
provided for in foundling hospitals, by cooking
and eating them. This was an extravaganza,
though really bolder and more coarsely practical
than mine, which did not provoke any reproaches
even to a dignitary of the supreme Irish church; its
own monstrosity was its excuse; mere extravagance was felt to license and accredit the little *jeu
d'esprit*, precisely as the blank impossibilities of
Lilliput, of Laputa, of the Yahoos, &c., had li-
censed those. If, therefore, any man thinks it
worth his while to tilt against so mere a foam-
bubble of gaiety as this lecture on the aesthetics of

murder, I shelter myself for the moment under the Telamonian shield of the Dean. But, in reality, my own little paper may plead a privileged excuse for its extravagance, such as is altogether wanting to the Dean's. Nobody can pretend, for a moment, on behalf of the Dean, that there is any ordinary and natural tendency in human thoughts, which could ever turn to infants as articles of diet; under any conceivable circumstances, this would be felt as the most aggravated form of cannibalism—cannibalism applying itself to the most defenceless part of the species. But, on the other hand, the tendency to a critical or aesthetic valuation of fires and murders is universal. If you are summoned to the spectacle of a great fire, undoubtedly the first impulse is—to assist in putting it out. But that field of exertion is very limited, and is soon filled by regular professional people, trained and equipped for the service. In the case of a fire which is operating upon *private* property, pity for a neighbor's calamity checks us at first in treating the affair as a scenic spectacle. But perhaps the fire may be confined to public buildings. And in any case, after we have paid our tribute of regret to the affair, considered as a calamity, inevitably, and without restraint, we go on to consider it as a stage spectacle. Exclamations of—How grand! How magnificent! arise in a sort of rapture from the crowd. For instance, when Drury Lane was burned down in the first decennium of this century, the falling in of the roof was signalized by a mimic suicide of the protecting Apollo that surmounted and crested the centre of this roof. The god was stationary with his lyre, and seemed looking down upon the fiery ruins that were so rapidly approaching him. Suddenly the supporting timbers below him gave way; a convulsive heave of the billowing flames seemed for a moment to raise the statue; and then, as if on some impulse of despair, the presiding deity appeared not to fall, but to throw himself into the fiery deluge, for he went down head foremost; and in all respects, the descent had the air of a voluntary act. What followed? From every one of the bridges over the river, and from other open areas which commanded the spectacle, there arose a sustained uproar of admiration and sympathy. Some few years before this event, a prodigious fire occurred at Liverpool; the *Goree*, a vast pile of warehouses close to one of the docks, was burned to the ground. The huge edifice, eight or nine stories high, and laden with most combustible goods, many thousand bales of cotton, wheat and oats in thousands of quarters, tar, turpentine, rum, gunpowder, &c., continued through many hours of darkness to feed this tremendous fire. To aggravate the calamity, it blew a regular gale of wind; luckily for the shipping, it blew inland, that is, to the east; and all the way down to Warrington, eighteen miles distant to the eastward, the whole

air was illuminated by flakes of cotton, often satu-
rated with rum, and by what seemed absolute
worlds of blazing sparks, that lighted up all the
upper chambers of the air. All the cattle lying
abroad in the fields through a breadth of eighteen
miles, were thrown into terror and agitation. Men,
of course, read in this hurrying overhead of scin-
tillating and blazing vortices, the annunciation of
some gigantic calamity going on in Liverpool; and
the lamentation on that account was universal.
But that mood of public sympathy did not at all
interfere to suppress or even to check the momen-
tary bursts of rapturous admiration, as this ar-
rowy sleet of many-colored fire rode on the wings
of hurricane, alternately through open depths of
air, or through dark clouds overhead.

Precisely the same treatment is applied to murders. After the first tribute of sorrow to those who
have perished, but, at all events, after the personal
interests have been tranquillized by time, inevitably the scenical features (what aesthetically
may be called the comparative *advantages*) of the
several murders are reviewed and valued. One
murder is compared with another; and the circumstances of superiority, as, for example, in the
incidence and effects of surprise, of mystery, &c.,
are collated and appraised. I, therefore, for *my* extravagance, claim an inevitable and perpetual
ground in the spontaneous tendencies of the
human mind when left to itself. But no one will

pretend that any corresponding plea can be advanced on behalf of Swift.

In this important distinction between myself and the Dean, lies one reason which prompted the present writing. A second purpose of this paper is, to make the reader acquainted circumstantially with three memorable cases of murder, which long ago the voice of amateurs has crowned with laurel, but especially with the two earliest of the three, viz., the immortal Williams' murders of 1812. The act and the actor are each separately in the highest degree interesting; and, as forty-two years have elapsed since 1812, it cannot be supposed that either is known circumstantially to the men of the current generation.

Never, throughout the annals of universal Christendom, has there indeed been any act of one solitary insulated individual, armed with power so appalling over the hearts of men, as that exterminating murder, by which, during the winter of 1812, John Williams in one hour, smote two houses with emptiness, exterminated all but two entire households, and asserted his own supremacy above all the children of Cain. It would be absolutely impossible adequately to describe the frenzy of feelings which, throughout the next fortnight, mastered the popular heart; the mere delirium of indignant horror in some, the mere delirium of panic in others. For twelve succeeding days, under some groundless notion that the unknown murderer had quitted London, the panic which had convulsed the mighty metropolis diffused itself all over the island. I was myself at that time nearly three hundred miles from London; but there, and everywhere, the panic was indescribable. One lady, my next neighbor, whom personally I knew, living at the moment, during the absence of her husband, with a few servants in a very solitary house, never rested until she had placed eighteen doors (so she told me, and, indeed, satisfied me by ocular proof), each secured by ponderous bolts, and bars, and chains, between her own bedroom and any intruder of human build. To reach her, even in her drawing-room, was like going, as a flag of truce, into a beleaguered fortress; at every sixth step one was stopped by a sort of portcullis. The panic was not confined to the rich; women in the humblest ranks more than once died upon the spot, from the shock attending some suspicious attempts at intrusion upon the part of vagrants, meditating probably nothing worse than a robbery, but whom the poor women, misled by the London newspapers, had fancied to be the dreadful London murderer. Meantime, this solitary artist, that rested in the centre of London, self-supported by his own conscious grandeur, as a domestic Attila, or 'scourge of God;' this man, that walked in darkness, and relied upon murder (as afterwards transpired) for bread, for clothes, for promotion in life, was silently preparing an effectual answer to the public journals; and on the twelfth day after his inaugural murder, he advertised his presence in London, and published to all men the absurdity of ascribing to *him* any ruralizing propensities, by striking a second blow, and accomplishing a second family extermination. Somewhat lightened was the *provincial* panic by this proof that the murderer had not condescended to sneak into the country, or to abandon for a moment, under any motive of caution or fear, the great metropolitan *castra stativa* of gigantic crime, seated for ever on the Thames. In fact, the great artist disdained a provincial reputation; and he must have felt, as a case of ludicrous disproportion, the contrast between a country town or village, on the one hand, and, on the other, a work more lasting than brass —a [Greek: *chtaema es aei*]—a murder such in quality as any murder that *he* would condescend to own for a work turned out from his own *studio*.

Coleridge, whom I saw some months after these terrific murders, told me, that, for *his* part, though at the time resident in London, he had not shared in the prevailing panic; *him* they effected only as a philosopher, and threw him into a profound reverie upon the tremendous power which is laid open in a moment to any man who can reconcile himself to the abjuration of all conscientious restraints, if, at the same time, thoroughly without fear. Not sharing in the public panic, however, Coleridge did not consider that panic at all unreasonable; for, as he said most truly in that vast metropolis there are many thousands of households, composed exclusively of women and children; many other thousands there are who necessarily confide their safety, in the long evenings, to the discretion of a young servant girl; and if she suffers herself to be beguiled by the pretence of a message from her mother, sister, or sweetheart, into opening the door, there, in one second of time, goes to wreck the security of the house. However, at that time, and for many months afterwards, the practice of steadily putting the chain upon the door before it was opened prevailed generally, and for a long time served as a record of that deep impression left upon London by Mr. Williams. Southey, I may add, entered deeply into the public feeling on this occasion, and said to me, within a week or two of the first murder, that it was a private event of that order which rose to the dignity of a national event. [1] But now, having prepared the reader to appreciate on its true scale this dreadful tissue of murder (which as a record belonging to an era that is now left forty-two years behind us, not one person in four of this generation can be expected to know correctly), let me pass to the circumstantial details of the affair.

Yet, first of all, one word as to the local scene of the murders. Ratcliffe Highway is a public thoroughfare in a most chaotic quarter of eastern or nautical London; and at this time (viz., in 1812), when no adequate police existed except the *detective* police of Bow Street, admirable for its own peculiar purposes, but utterly incommensurate to the general service of the capital, it was a most dangerous quarter. Every third man at the least might be set down as a foreigner. Lascars, Chinese, Moors, Negroes, were met at every step. And apart from the manifold ruffianism, shrouded impenetrably under the mixed hats and turbans of men whose past was untraceable to any European eye, it is well known that the navy (especially, in time of war, the commercial navy) of Christendom is the sure receptacle of all the murderers and ruffians whose crimes have given them a motive for withdrawing themselves for a season from the public eye. It is true, that few of this class are qualified to act as 'able' seamen: but at all times, and especially during war, only a small proportion (or *nucleus*) of each ship's company consists of such men: the large majority being mere untutored landsmen. John Williams, however, who had been occasionally rated as a seaman on board of various Indiamen, &c., was probably a very accomplished seaman. Pretty generally, in fact, he was a ready and adroit man, fertile in resources under all sudden difficulties, and most flexibly adapting himself to all varieties of social life. Williams was a man of middle stature (five feet seven and a-half, to five feet eight inches high), slenderly built, rather thin, but wiry, tolerably muscular, and clear of all superfluous flesh. A lady, who saw him under examination (I think at the Thames Police Office), assured me that his hair was of the most extraordinary and vivid color, viz., bright yellow, something between an orange and lemon color. Williams had been in India; chiefly in Bengal and Madras: but he had also been upon the Indus. Now, it is notorious that, in the Punjaub, horses of a high caste are often painted—crimson, blue, green, purple; and it struck me that Williams might, for some casual purpose of disguise, have taken a hint from this practice of Scinde and Lahore, so that the color might not have been natural. In other respects, his appearance was natural enough; and, judging by a plaster cast of him, which I purchased in London, I should say mean, as regarded his facial structure. One fact, however, was striking, and fell in with the impression of his natural tiger character, that his face wore at all times a bloodless ghastly pallor. 'You might imagine,' said my informant, 'that in his veins circulated not red life-blood, such as could kindle into the blush of shame, of wrath, of pity— but a green sap that welled from no human heart.' His eyes seemed frozen and glazed, as if their light were all converged upon some victim lurking in the far background. So far his appearance might have repelled; but, on the other hand, the concurrent testimony of many witnesses, and also the silent testimony of facts, showed that the oiliness and snaky insinuation of his demeanor counteracted the repulsiveness of his ghastly face, and amongst inexperienced young women won for him a very favorable reception. In particular, one gentle-mannered girl, whom Williams had undoubtedly designed to murder, gave in evidence—that once, when sitting alone with her, he had said, 'Now, Miss R., supposing that I should appear about midnight at your bedside, armed with a carving knife, what would you say?' To which the confiding girl had, replied, 'Oh, Mr. Williams, if it was anybody else, I should be frightened. But, as soon as I heard *your* voice, I should be tranquil.' Poor girl! had this outline sketch of Mr. Williams been filled in and realized, she would have seen something in the corpse-like face, and heard something in the sinister voice, that would have unsettled her tranquillity for ever. But nothing short of such dreadful experiences could avail to unmask Mr. John Williams.

Into this perilous region it was that, on a Saturday night in December, Mr. Williams, whom we suppose to have long since made his *coup d'essai*, forced his way through the crowded streets, bound on business. To say, was to do. And this night he had said to himself secretly, that he would execute a design which he had already

sketched, and which, when finished, was destined
on the following day to strike consternation into
'all that mighty heart' of London, from centre to
circumference. It was afterwards remembered that
he had quitted his lodgings on this dark errand
about eleven o'clock P. M.; not that he meant to
begin so soon: but he needed to reconnoitre. He
carried his tools closely buttoned up under his
loose roomy coat. It was in harmony with the general subtlety of his character, and his polished ha-
tred of brutality, that by universal agreement his
manners were distinguished for exquisite suavity:
the tiger's heart was masked by the most insinuating and snaky refinement. All his acquaintances
afterwards described his dissimulation as so ready
and so perfect, that if, in making his way through
the streets, always so crowded on a Saturday
night in neighborhoods so poor, he had accidentally jostled any person, he would (as they were
all satisfied) have stopped to offer the most gentle-
manly apologies: with his devilish heart brooding
over the most hellish of purposes, he would yet
have paused to express a benign hope that the
huge mallet, buttoned up under his elegant
surtout, with a view to the little business that
awaited him about ninety minutes further on, had
not inflicted any pain on the stranger with whom
he had come into collision. Titian, I believe, but
certainly Rubens, and perhaps Vandyke, made it a
rule never to practise his art but in full dress—

point ruffles, bag wig, and diamond-hilted sword; and Mr. Williams, there is reason to believe, when he went out for a grand compound massacre (in another sense, one might have applied to it the Oxford phrase of *going out as Grand Compounder*), always assumed black silk stockings and pumps; nor would he on any account have degraded his position as an artist by wearing a morning gown. In his second great performance, it was particularly noticed and recorded by the one sole trembling man, who under killing agonies of fear was compelled (as the reader will find) from a secret stand to become the solitary spectator of his atrocities, that Mr. Williams wore a long blue frock, of the very finest cloth, and richly lined with silk. Amongst the anecdotes which circulated about him, it was also said at the time, that Mr. Williams employed the first of dentists, and also the first of chiropodists. On no account would he patronize any second-rate skill. And beyond a doubt, in that perilous little branch of business which was practised by himself, he might be regarded as the most aristocratic and fastidious of artists.

But who meantime was the victim, to whose abode he was hurrying? For surely he never could be so indiscreet as to be sailing about on a roving cruise in search of some chance person to murder? Oh, no: he had suited himself with a victim some time before, viz., an old and very intimate friend. For he seems to have laid it down as a maxim—

that the best person to murder was a friend; and, in default of a friend, which is an article one cannot always command, an acquaintance: because, in either case, on first approaching his subject, suspicion would be disarmed: whereas a stranger might take alarm, and find in the very countenance of his murderer elect a warning summons to place himself on guard. However, in the present ease, his destined victim was supposed to unite both characters: originally he had been a friend; but subsequently, on good cause arising, he had become an enemy. Or more probably, as others said, the feelings had long since languished which gave life to either relation of friendship or of enmity. Marr was the name of that unhappy man, who (whether in the character of friend or enemy) had been selected for the subject of this present Saturday night's performance. And the story current at that time about the connection between Williams and Marr, having (whether true or not true) never been contradicted upon authority, was, that they sailed in the same Indiaman to Calcutta; that they had quarrelled when at sea; but another version of the story said—no: they had quarrelled after returning from sea; and the subject of their quarrel was Mrs. Marr, a very pretty young woman, for whose favor they had been rival candidates, and at one time with most bitter enmity towards each other. Some circumstances give a color of probability to this story. Otherwise it has sometimes happened, on occasion of a murder not sufficiently accounted for, that, from pure goodness of heart intolerant of a mere sordid motive for a striking murder, some person has forged, and the public has accredited, a story representing the murderer as having moved under some loftier excitement: and in this case the public, too much shocked at the idea of Williams having on the single motive of gain consummated so complex a tragedy, welcomed the tale which represented him as governed by deadly malice, growing out of the more impassioned and noble rivalry for the favor of a woman. The case remains in some degree doubtful; but, certainly, the probability is, that Mrs. Marr had been the true cause, the *causa teterrima*, of the feud between the men. Meantime, the minutes are numbered, the sands of the hour-glass are running out, that measure the duration of this feud upon earth. This night it shall cease. To-morrow is the day which in England they call Sunday, which in Scotland they call by the Judaic name of 'Sabbath.' To both nations, under different names, the day has the same functions; to both it is a day of rest. For thee also, Marr, it shall be a day of rest; so is it written; thou, too, young Marr, shalt find rest—thou, and thy household, and the stranger that is within thy gates. But that rest must be in the world which lies beyond the grave. On this side the grave ye have all slept your final sleep.

The night was one of exceeding darkness; and in this humble quarter of London, whatever the night happened to be, light or dark, quiet or stormy, all shops were kept open on Saturday nights until twelve o'clock, at the least, and many for half an hour longer. There was no rigorous and pedantic Jewish superstition about the exact limits of Sunday. At the very worst, the Sunday stretched over from one o'clock, A. M. of one day, up to eight o'clock A. M. of the next, making a clear circuit of thirty-one hours. This, surely, was long enough. Marr, on this particular Saturday night, would be content if it were even shorter, provided it would come more quickly, for he has been toiling through sixteen hours behind his counter. Marr's position in life was this: he kept a little hosier's shop, and had invested in his stock and the fittings of his shop about 180 pounds. Like all men engaged in trade, he suffered some anxieties. He was a new beginner; but, already, bad debts had alarmed him; and bills were coming to maturity that were not likely to be met by commensurate sales. Yet, constitutionally, he was a sanguine hoper. At this time he was a stout, fresh-colored young man of twenty-seven; in some slight degree uneasy from his commercial prospects, but still cheerful, and anticipating— (how vainly!)—that for this night, and the next night, at least, he will rest his wearied head and his cares upon the faithful bosom of his sweet lovely young wife. The household of Marr, consisting of five persons, is as follows: First, there is himself, who, if he should happen to be ruined, in a limited commercial sense, has energy enough to jump up again, like a pyramid of fire, and soar high above ruin many times repeated. Yes, poor Marr, so it might be, if thou wert left to thy native energies unmolested; but even now there stands on the other side of the street one born of hell, who puts his peremptory negative on all these flattering prospects. Second in the list of his household, stands his pretty and amiable wife, who is happy after the fashion of youthful wives, for she is only twenty-two, and anxious (if at all) only on account of her darling infant. For, thirdly, there is in a cradle, not quite nine feet below the street, viz., in a warm, cosy kitchen, and rocked at intervals by the young mother, a baby eight months old. Nineteen months have Marr and herself been married; and this is their first-born child. Grieve not for this child, that it must keep the deep rest of Sunday in some other world; for wherefore should an orphan, steeped to the lips in poverty, when once bereaved of father and mother, linger upon an alien and murderous earth? Fourthly, there is a stoutish boy, an apprentice, say thirteen years old; a Devonshire boy, with handsome features, such as most Devonshire youths have; [2] satisfied with his place; not overworked; treated kindly, and aware that he was treated kindly, by his master and mistress. Fifthly, and lastly, bringing up the rear of this quiet household, is a servant girl, a grown-up young woman; and she, being particularly kind-hearted, occupied (as often happens in families of humble pretensions as to rank) a sort of sisterly place in her relation to her mistress. A great democratic change is at this very time (1854), and has been for twenty years, passing over British society. Multitudes of persons are becoming ashamed of saying, 'my master,' or 'my mistress:' the term now in the slow process of superseding it is, 'my employer.' Now, in the United States, such an expression of democratic hauteur, though disagreeable as a needless proclamation of independence which nobody is disputing, leaves, however, no lasting bad effect. For the domestic 'helps' are pretty generally in a state of transition so sure and so rapid to the headship of domestic establishments belonging to themselves, that in effect they are but ignoring, for the present moment, a relation which would at any rate dissolve itself in a year or two. But in England, where no such resources exist of everlasting surplus lands, the tendency of the change is painful. It carries with it a sullen and a coarse expression of immunity from a yoke which was in any case a light one, and often a benign one. In some other place I will illustrate my meaning. Here, apparently, in Mrs. Marr's service, the principle concerned illustrated itself practically. Mary, the female servant, felt a sincere and unaffected respect for a mistress whom she saw so steadily occupied with her domestic duties, and who, though so young, and invested with some slight authority, never exerted it capriciously, or even showed it at all conspiciously. According to the testimony of all the neighbors, she treated her mistress with a shade of unobtrusive respect on the one hand, and yet was eager to relieve her, whenever that was possible, from the weight of her maternal duties, with the cheerful voluntary service of a sister.

To this young woman it was, that, suddenly, within three or four minutes of midnight, Marr called aloud from the head of the stairs—directing her to go out and purchase some oysters for the family supper. Upon what slender accidents hang oftentimes solemn lifelong results! Marr occupied in the concerns of his shop, Mrs. Marr occupied with some little ailment and restlessness of her baby, had both forgotten the affair of supper; the time was now narrowing every moment, as regarded any variety of choice; and oysters were perhaps ordered as the likeliest article to be had at all, after twelve o'clock should have struck. And yet, upon this trivial circumstance depended Mary's life. Had she been sent abroad for supper at the ordinary time of ten or eleven o'clock, it is almost certain that she, the solitary member of the household who escaped from the exterminating tragedy, would *not* have escaped; too surely she would have shared the general fate. It had now become necessary to be quick. Hastily, therefore, receiving money from Marr with a basket in her hand, but unbonneted, Mary tripped out of the shop. It became afterwards, on recollection, a heart-chilling remembrance to herself—that, precisely as she emerged from the shop-door, she noticed, on the opposite side of the street, by the light of the lamps, a man's figure; stationary at the instant, but in the next instant slowly moving. This was Williams; as a little incident, either just before or just after (at present it is impossible to say which), sufficiently proved. Now, when one considers the inevitable hurry and trepidation of Mary under the circumstances stated, time barely sufficing for any chance of executing her errand, it becomes evident that she must have connected some deep feeling of mysterious uneasiness with the movements of this unknown man; else, assuredly, she would not have found her attention disposable for such a case. Thus far, she herself threw some little light upon what it might be that, semi- consciously, was then passing through her mind; she said, that, notwithstanding the darkness, which would not permit her to trace the man's features, or to ascertain the exact direction of his eyes, it yet struck her, that from his carriage when in motion, and from the apparent inclination of his person, he must be looking at No. 29.

The little incident which I have alluded to as confirming Mary's belief was, that, at some period not very far from midnight, the watchman had specially noticed this stranger; he had observed him continually peeping into the window of Marr's shop; and had thought this act, connected with the man's appearance, so suspicious, that he stepped into Marr's shop, and communicated what he had seen. This fact he afterwards stated before the magistrates; and he added, that subsequently, viz., a few minutes after twelve (eight or ten minutes, probably, after the departure of Mary), he (the watchman), when re-entering upon his ordinary half-hourly beat, was requested by Marr to assist him in closing the shutters. Here they had a final communication with each other; and the watchman mentioned to Marr that the mysterious stranger had now apparently taken himself off; for that he had not been visible since the first communication made to Marr by the watchman. There is little doubt that Williams had observed the watchman's visit to Marr, and had thus had his attention seasonably drawn to the indiscretion of his own demeanor; so that the warning, given unavailingly to Marr, had been turned to account by Williams. There can be still less doubt, that the bloodhound had commenced his work within one minute of the watchman's assisting Marr to put up his shutters. And on the following consideration:—that which prevented

Williams from commencing even earlier, was the exposure of the shop's whole interior to the gaze of street passengers. It was indispensable that the shutters should be accurately closed before Williams could safely get to work. But, as soon as ever this preliminary precaution had been completed, once having secured that concealment from the public eye it then became of still greater importance not to lose a moment by delay, than previously it had been not to hazard any thing by precipitance. For all depended upon going in before Marr should have locked the door. On any other mode of effecting an entrance (as, for instance, by waiting for the return of Mary, and making his entrance simultaneously with her), it will be seen that Williams must have forfeited that particular advantage which mute facts, when read into their true construction, will soon show the reader that he must have employed. Williams waited, of necessity, for the sound of the watchman's retreating steps; waited, perhaps, for thirty seconds; but when that danger was past, the next danger was, lest Marr should lock the door; one turn of the key, and the murderer would have been locked out. In, therefore, he bolted, and by a dexterous movement of his left hand, no doubt, turned the key, without letting Marr perceive this fatal stratagem. It is really wonderful and most interesting to pursue the successive steps of this monster, and to notice the absolute certainty with which the silent hieroglyphics of the case betray to us the whole process and movements of the bloody drama, not less surely and fully than if we had been ourselves hidden in Marr's shop, or had looked down from the heavens of mercy upon this hell-kite, that knew not what mercy meant. That he had concealed from Marr his trick, secret and rapid, upon the lock, is evident; because else, Marr would instantly have taken the alarm, especially after what the watchman had communicated. But it will soon be seen that Marr had *not* been alarmed. In reality, towards the full success of Williams, it was important, in the last degree, to intercept and forestall any yell or shout of agony from Marr. Such an outcry, and in a situation so slenderly fenced off from the street, viz., by walls the very thinnest, makes itself heard outside pretty nearly as well as if it were uttered in the street. Such an outcry it was indispensable to stifle. It *was* stifled; and the reader will soon understand *how*. Meantime, at this point, let us leave the murderer alone with his victims. For fifty minutes let him work his pleasure. The front-door, as we know, is now fastened against all help. Help there is none. Let us, therefore, in vision, attach ourselves to Mary; and, when all is over, let us come back with *her*, again raise the curtain, and read the dreadful record of all that has passed in her absence.

The poor girl, uneasy in her mind to an extent

that she could but half understand, roamed up and down in search of an oyster shop; and finding none that was still open, within any circuit that her ordinary experience had made her acquainted with, she fancied it best to try the chances of some remoter district. Lights she saw gleaming or twinkling at a distance, that still tempted her onwards; and thus, amongst unknown streets poorly lighted, [3] and on a night of peculiar darkness, and in a region of London where ferocious tumults were continually turning her out of what seemed to be the direct course, naturally she got bewildered. The purpose with which she started, had by this time become hopeless. Nothing remained for her now but to retrace her steps. But this was difficult; for she was afraid to ask directions from chance passengers, whose appearance the darkness prevented her from reconnoitring. At length by his lantern she recognized a watchman; through him she was guided into the right road; and in ten minutes more, she found herself back at the door of No. 29, in Ratcliffe Highway. But by this time she felt satisfied that she must have been absent for fifty or sixty minutes; indeed, she had heard, at a distance, the cry of *past one o'clock*, which, commencing a few seconds after one, lasted intermittingly for ten or thirteen minutes.

In the tumult of agonizing thoughts that very soon surprised her, naturally it became hard for her to recall distinctly the whole succession of doubts, and jealousies, and shadowy misgivings that soon opened upon her. But, so far as could be collected, she had not in the first moment of reaching home noticed anything decisively alarming. In very many cities bells are the main instruments for communicating between the street and the interior of houses: but in London knockers prevail. At Marr's there was both a knocker and a bell. Mary rang, and at the same time very gently knocked. She had no fear of disturbing her master or mistress; *them* she made sure of finding still up. Her anxiety was for the baby, who being disturbed, might again rob her mistress of a night's rest. And she well knew that, with three people all anxiously awaiting her return, and by this time, perhaps, seriously uneasy at her delay, the least audible whisper from herself would in a moment bring one of them to the door. Yet how is this? To her astonishment, but with the astonishment came creeping over her an icy horror, no stir nor murmur was heard ascending from the kitchen. At this moment came back upon her, with shuddering anguish, the indistinct image of the stranger in the loose dark coat, whom she had seen stealing along under the shadowy lamplight, and too certainly watching her master's motions: keenly she now reproached herself that, under whatever stress of hurry, she had not acquainted Mr. Marr with the suspicious appearances. Poor girl! she did not then know that, if this communication could have availed to put Marr upon his guard, it had reached him from another quarter; so that her own omission, which had in reality arisen under her hurry to execute her master's commission, could not be charged with any bad consequences. But all such reflections this way or that were swallowed up at this point in over-mastering panic. That her double summons *could* have been unnoticed—this solitary fact in one moment made a revelation of horror. One person might have fallen asleep, but two—but three—*that* was a mere impossibility. And even supposing all three together with the baby locked in sleep, still how unaccountable was this utter—utter silence! Most naturally at this moment something like hysterical horror overshadowed the poor girl, and now at last she rang the bell with the violence that belongs to sickening terror. This done, she paused: self-command enough she still retained, though fast and fast it was slipping away from her, to bethink herself—that, if any overwhelming accident *had* compelled both Marr and his apprentice-boy to leave the house in order to summon surgical aid from opposite quarters—a thing barely supposable—still, even in that case Mrs. Marr and her infant would be left; and some murmuring reply, under any extremity, would be elicited from the poor mother. To pause, therefore, to impose stern silence upon herself, so as to leave room for the possible answer to this final appeal, became a duty of spasmodic effort. Listen, therefore, poor trembling heart; listen, and for twenty seconds be still as death. Still as death she was: and during that dreadful stillness, when she hushed her breath that she might listen, occurred an incident of killing fear, that to her dying day would never cease to renew its echoes in her ear. She, Mary, the poor trembling girl, checking and overruling herself by a final effort, that she might leave full opening for her dear young mistress's answer to her own last frantic appeal, heard at last and most distinctly a sound within the house. Yes, now beyond a doubt there is coming an answer to her summons. What was it? On the stairs, not the stairs that led downwards to the kitchen, but the stairs that led upwards to the single story of bed-chambers above, was heard a creaking sound. Next was heard most distinctly a footfall: one, two, three, four, five stairs were slowly and distinctly descended. Then the dreadful footsteps were heard advancing along the little narrow passage to the door. The steps—oh heavens! *whose* steps?—have paused at the door. The very breathing can be heard of that dreadful being, who has silenced all breathing except his own in the house. There is but a door between him and Mary. What is he doing on the other side of the door? A cautious step, a stealthy step it was that came down the stairs, then paced along the little narrow passage—narrow as a coffin—till at last the step pauses at the door. How hard the fellow breathes! He, the solitary murderer, is on one side the door; Mary is on the other side. Now, suppose that he should suddenly open the door, and that incautiously in the dark Mary should rush in, and find herself in the arms of the murderer. Thus far the case is a possible one—that to a certainty, had this little trick been tried immediately upon Mary's return, it would have succeeded; had the door been opened suddenly upon her first tingle-tingle, headlong she would have tumbled in, and perished. But now Mary is upon her guard. The unknown murderer and she have both their lips upon the door, listening, breathing hard; but luckily they are on different sides of the door; and upon the least indication of unlocking or unlatching, she would have recoiled into the asylum of general darkness.

What was the murderer's meaning in coming along the passage to the front door? The meaning was this: separately, as an individual, Mary was worth nothing at all to him. But, considered as a member of a household, she had this value, viz., that she, if caught and murdered, perfected and rounded the desolation of the house. The case being reported, as reported it would be all over Christendom, led the imagination captive. The whole covey of victims was thus netted; the household ruin was thus full and orbicular; and in that proportion the tendency of men and women, flutter as they might, would be helplessly and hopelessly to sink into the all-conquering hands of the mighty murderer. He had but to say—my testimonials are dated from No. 29 Ratcliffe Highway, and the poor vanquished imagination sank powerless before the fascinating rattlesnake eye of the murderer. There is not a doubt that the motive of the murderer for standing on the inner side of Marr's front-door, whilst Mary stood on the outside, was—a hope that, if he quietly opened the door, whisperingly counterfeiting Marr's voice, and saying, What made you stay so long? possibly she might have been inveigled. He was wrong; the time was past for that; Mary was now maniacally awake; she began now to ring the bell and to ply the knocker with unintermitting violence. And the natural consequence was, that the next door neighbor, who had recently gone to bed and instantly fallen asleep, was roused; and by the incessant violence of the ringing and the knocking, which now obeyed a delirious and uncontrollable impulse in Mary, he became sensible that some very dreadful event must be at the root of so clamorous an uproar. To rise, to throw up the sash, to demand angrily the cause of this unseasonable tumult, was the work of a moment. The poor girl remained sufficiently mistress of herself rapidly to explain the circumstance of her own absence for an hour; her belief that Mr. and Mrs. Marr's family had all been murdered in the interval; and that at this very moment the murderer was in the house.

The person to whom she addressed this statement was a pawnbroker; and a thoroughly brave man he must have been; for it was a perilous undertaking, merely as a trial of physical strength, singly to face a mysterious assassin, who had apparently signalized his prowess by a triumph so comprehensive. But, again, for the imagination it required an effort of self-conquest to rush headlong into the presence of one invested with a cloud of mystery, whose nation, age, motives, were all alike unknown. Rarely on any field of battle has a soldier been called upon to face so complex a danger. For if the entire family of his neighbor Marr had been exterminated, were this indeed true, such a scale of bloodshed would seem to argue that there must have been two persons as the perpetrators; or if one singly had accomplished such a ruin, in that case how colossal must have been his audacity! probably, also, his skill and animal power! Moreover, the unknown enemy (whether single or double) would, doubtless, be elaborately armed. Yet, under all these disadvantages, did this fearless man rush at once to the field of butchery in his neighbor's house. Waiting only to draw on his trousers, and to arm himself with the kitchen poker, he went down into his own little back-yard. On this mode of approach, he would have a chance of intercepting the murderer; whereas from the front there would be no such chance; and there would also be considerable delay in the process of breaking open the door. A brick wall, nine or ten feet high, divided his own back premises from those of Marr. Over this he vaulted; and at the moment when he was recalling himself to the necessity of going back for a candle, he suddenly perceived a feeble ray of light already glimmering on some part of Marr's premises. Marr's back-door stood wide open. Probably the murderer had passed through it one half minute before. Rapidly the brave man passed onwards to the shop, and there beheld the carnage of the night stretched out on the floor, and the narrow premises so floated with gore, that it was hardly possible to escape the pollution of blood in picking out a path to the front-door. In the lock of the door still remained the key which had given to the unknown murderer so fatal an advantage over his victims. By this time, the heart- shaking news involved in the outcries of Mary (to whom it occurred that by possibility some one out of so many victims might still be within the reach of medical aid, but that all would depend upon speed) had availed, even at that late hour, to gather a small mob about the house. The pawnbroker threw open the door. One or two watchmen headed the crowd; but the soul-harrowing spectacle checked them, and impressed sudden silence upon their voices, previously so loud. The tragic drama read aloud its own history, and the succession of its several steps—few and summary. The murderer was as yet altogether unknown; not even suspected. But there were reasons for thinking that he must have been a person familiarly known to Marr. He had entered the shop by opening the door after it had been closed by Marr. But it was justly argued—that, after the caution conveyed to Marr by the watchman, the appearance of any stranger in the shop at that hour, and in so dangerous a neighborhood, and entering by so irregular and suspicious a course, (*i.e.*, walking in after the door had been closed, and after the closing of the shutters had cut off all open communication with the street), would naturally have roused Marr to an attitude of vigilance and self-defence. Any indication, therefore, that Marr had *not* been so roused, would argue to a certainty that *something* had occurred to neutralize this alarm, and fatally to disarm the prudent jealousies of Marr. But this 'something' could only have lain in one simple fact, viz., that the person of the murderer was familiarly known to Marr as that of an ordinary and unsuspected acquaintance. This being presupposed as the key to all the rest, the whole course and evolution of the subsequent drama becomes clear as daylight. The murderer, it is evident, had opened gently, and again closed behind him with equal gentleness, the street-door. He had then advanced to the little counter, all the while exchanging the ordinary salutation of an old acquaintance with the unsuspecting Marr. Having reached the counter, he would then ask Marr for a pair of unbleached cotton socks. In a shop so small as Marr's, there could be no great latitude of choice for disposing of the different commodities. The arrangement of these had no doubt become familiar to the murderer; and he had already ascertained that, in order to reach down the particular parcel wanted at present, Marr would find it requisite to face round to the rear, and, at the same moment, to raise his eyes and his hands to a level eighteen inches above his own head. This movement placed him in the most disadvantageous possible position with regard to the murderer, who now, at the instant when Marr's hands and eyes were embarrassed, and the back of his head fully exposed, suddenly from below his large surtout, had unslung a heavy ship-carpenter's mallet, and, with one solitary blow, had so thoroughly stunned his victim, as to leave him incapable of resistance. The whole position of Marr told its own tale. He had collapsed naturally behind the counter, with his hands so occupied as to confirm the whole outline of the affair as I have here suggested it. Probable enough it is that the very first blow, the first indication of treachery that reached Marr, would also be the last blow as regarded the abolition of consciousness. The murderer's plan and *rationale* of murder started systematically from this infliction of apoplexy, or at least of a stunning sufficient to insure a long loss of consciousness. This opening step placed the murderer at his ease. But still, as returning sense might constantly have led to the fullest exposures, it was his settled practice, by way of consummation, to cut the throat. To one invariable type all the murders on this occasion conformed: the skull was first shattered; this step secured the murderer from instant retaliation; and then, by way of locking up all into eternal silence, uniformly the throat was cut. The rest of the circumstances, as self-revealed, were these. The fall of Marr might, probably enough, cause a dull, confused sound of a scuffle, and the more so, as it could not now be confounded with any street uproar—the shop-door being shut. It is more probable, however, that the signal for the alarm passing down to the kitchen, would arise when the murderer proceeded to cut Marr's throat. The very confined situation behind the counter would render it impossible, under the critical hurry of the case, to expose the throat broadly; the horrid scene would proceed by partial and interrupted cuts; deep groans would arise; and then would come the rush up-stairs. Against this, as the only dangerous stage in the transaction, the murderer would have specially prepared. Mrs. Marr and the apprentice-boy, both young and active, would make, of course, for the street door; had Mary been at home, and three persons at once had combined to distract the purposes of the murderer, it is barely possible that one of them would have succeeded in reaching the street. But the dreadful swing of the heavy mallet intercepted both the boy and his mistress before they could reach the door. Each of them lay stretched out on the centre of the shop floor; and the very moment that this disabling was accomplished, the accursed hound was down upon their throats with his razor. The fact is, that, in the mere blindness of pity for poor Marr, on hearing his groans, Mrs. Marr had lost sight of her obvious policy; she and the boy ought to have made for the back door; the alarm would thus have been given in the open air; which, of itself, was a great point; and several means of distracting the murderer's attention offered upon that course, which the extreme limitation of the shop denied to them upon the other.

Vain would be all attempts to convey the horror which thrilled the gathering spectators of this piteous tragedy. It was known to the crowd that one person had, by some accident, escaped the general massacre: but she was now speechless, and probably delirious; so that, in compassion for her pitiable situation, one female neighbor had carried her away, and put her to bed. Hence it had happened, for a longer space of time than could else have been possible, that no person present was sufficiently acquainted with the Marrs to be aware of the little infant; for the bold pawnbroker had gone off to make a communication to the coroner; and another neighbor to lodge some evidence which he thought urgent at a neighboring police-office. Suddenly some person appeared amongst the crowd who was aware that the murdered parents had a young infant; this would be found either below-stairs, or in one of the bedrooms above. Immediately a stream of people poured down into the kitchen, where at once they saw the cradle—but with the bedclothes in a state of indescribable confusion. On disentangling these, pools of blood became visible; and the next ominous sign was, that the hood of the cradle had been smashed to pieces. It became evident that the wretch had found himself doubly embarrassed—first, by the arched hood at the head of the cradle, which, accordingly, he had beat into a ruin with his mallet, and secondly, by the gathering of the blankets and pillows about the baby's head. The free play of his blows had thus been baffled. And he had therefore finished the scene by applying his razor to the throat of the little innocent; after which, with no apparent purpose, as though he had become confused by the spectacle of his own atrocities, he had busied himself in piling the clothes elaborately over the child's corpse. This incident undeniably gave the character of a vindictive proceeding to the whole affair, and so far confirmed the current rumor that the quarrel between Williams and Marr had originated in rival-ship. One writer, indeed, alleged that the murderer might have found it necessary for his own safety to extinguish the crying of the child; but it was justly replied, that a child only eight months old could not have cried under any sense of the tragedy proceeding, but simply in its ordinary way for the absence of its mother; and such a cry, even if audible at all out of the house, must have been precisely what the neighbors were hearing constantly, so that it could have drawn no special attention, nor suggested any reasonable alarm to the murderer. No one incident, indeed, throughout the whole tissue of atrocities, so much envenomed the popular fury against the unknown ruffian, as this useless butchery of the infant.

Naturally, on the Sunday morning that dawned four or five hours later, the case was too full of horror not to diffuse itself in all directions; but I have no reason to think that it crept into any one of the numerous Sunday papers. In the regular course, any ordinary occurrence, not occurring, or not transpiring until fifteen minutes after 1 A. M. on a Sunday morning, would first reach the public ear through the Monday editions of the Sunday papers, and the regular morning papers of the Monday. But, if such were the course pursued on this occasion, never can there have been a more signal oversight. For it is certain, that to have met the public demand for details on the Sunday, which might so easily have been done by cancelling a couple of dull columns, and substituting a circumstantial narrative, for which the pawnbroker and the watchman could have furnished the materials, would have made a small fortune. By proper handbills dispersed through all quarters of the infinite metropolis, two hundred and fifty thousand extra copies might have been sold; that is, by any journal that should have collected *exclusive* materials, meeting the public excitement, everywhere stirred to the centre by flying rumors, and everywhere burning for ampler information. On the Sunday se'ennight (Sunday the *octave* from the event), took place the funeral of the Marrs; in the first coffin was placed Marr; in the second Mrs. Marr, and the baby in her arms; in the third the apprentice boy. They were buried side by side; and thirty thousand laboring people followed the funeral procession, with horror and grief written in their countenances.

As yet no whisper was astir that indicated, even conjecturally, the hideous author of these ruins—this patron of grave-diggers. Had as much been known on this Sunday of the funeral concerning that person as became known universally six days later, the people would have gone right from the churchyard to the murderer's lodgings, and (brooking no delay) would have torn him limb from limb. As yet, however, in mere default of any object on whom reasonable suspicion could settle, the public wrath was compelled to suspend itself. Else, far indeed from showing any tendency to subside, the public emotion strengthened every day conspicuously, as the reverberation of the shock began to travel back from the provinces to the capital. On every great road in the kingdom, continual arrests were made of vagrants and 'trampers,' who could give no satisfactory account of themselves, or whose appearance in any respect answered to the imperfect description of Williams furnished by the watchman.

With this mighty tide of pity and indignation pointing backwards to the dreadful past, there mingled also in the thoughts of reflecting persons an under-current of fearful expectation for the immediate future. 'The earthquake,' to quote a fragment from a striking passage in Wordsworth—

'The earthquake is not satisfied at once.'

All perils, specially malignant, are recurrent. A murderer, who is such by passion and by a wolfish craving for bloodshed as a mode of unnatural luxury, cannot relapse into *inertia*. Such a man, even more than the Alpine chamois hunter, comes to crave the dangers and the hairbreadth escapes of his trade, as a condiment for seasoning the insipid monotonies of daily life. But, apart from the hellish instincts that might too surely be relied on for renewed atrocities, it was clear that the murderer of the Marrs, wheresoever lurking, must be a needy man; and a needy man of that class least likely to seek or to find resources in honorable modes of industry; for which, equally by haughty disgust and by disuse of the appropriate habits, men of violence are specially disqualified. Were it, therefore, merely for a livelihood, the murderer whom all hearts were yearning to decipher, might be expected to make his resurrection on some stage of horror, after a reasonable interval. Even in the Marr murder, granting that it had been governed chiefly by cruel and vindictive impulses, it was still clear that the desire of booty had co-operated with such feelings. Equally clear it was that this desire must have been disappointed: excepting the trivial sum reserved by Marr for the week's expenditure, the murderer found, doubtless, little or nothing that he could turn to account. Two guineas, perhaps, would be the outside of what he had obtained in the way of booty. A week or so would see the end of that. The conviction, therefore, of all people was, that in a month or two, when the fever of excitement might a little have cooled down, or have been superseded by other topics of fresher interest, so that the newborn vigilance of household life would have had time to relax, some new murder, equally appalling, might be counted upon.

Such was the public expectation. Let the reader then figure to himself the pure frenzy of horror when in this hush of expectation, looking, indeed, and waiting for the unknown arm to strike once more, but not believing that any audacity could be equal to such an attempt as yet, whilst all eyes were watching, suddenly, on the twelfth night from the Marr murder, a second case of the same mysterious nature, a murder on the same exterminating plan was perpetrated in the very same neighborhood. It was on the Thursday next but one succeeding to the Marr murder that this second atrocity took place; and many people thought at the time, that in its dramatic features of thrilling interest, this second case even went beyond the first. The family which suffered in this instance was that of a Mr. Williamson; and the house was situated, if not absolutely *in* Ratcliffe Highway, at any rate immediately round the corner of some secondary street, running at right angles to this public thoroughfare, Mr. Williamson was a well-known and respectable man, long settled in that district; he was supposed to be rich; and more with a view to the employment furnished by such a calling, than with much anxiety for further accumulations, he kept a sort of tavern; which, in this respect, might be considered on an old patriarchal footing—that, although people of considerable property resorted to the house in the evenings, no kind of anxious separation was maintained between them and the other visitors from the class of artisans or common laborers. Anybody who conducted himself with propriety was free to take a seat, and call for any liquor that he might prefer. And thus the society was pretty miscellaneous; in part stationary, but in some proportion fluctuating. The household consisted of the following five persons:—1. Mr. Williamson, its head, who was an old man above seventy, and was well fitted for his situation, being civil, and not at all morose, but, at the same time, firm in maintaining order; 2. Mrs. Williamson, his wife, about ten years younger than himself; 3. a little grand-daughter, about nine years old; 4. a housemaid, who was nearly forty years old; 5. a young journeyman, aged about twenty-six, belonging to some manufacturing establishment (of what class I have forgotten); neither do I remember of what nation he was. It was the established rule at Mr. Williamson's, that, exactly as the clock struck eleven, all the company, without favor or exception, moved off. That was one of the customs by which, in so stormy a district, Mr. Williamson had found it possible to keep his house free from brawls. On the present Thursday night everything had gone on as usual, except for one slight shadow of suspicion, which had caught the attention of more persons than one. Perhaps at a less agitating time it would hardly have been noticed; but now, when the first question and the last in all social meetings turned upon the Marrs, and their unknown murderer, it was a circumstance naturally fitted to cause some uneasiness, that a stranger, of sinister appearance, in a wide surtout, had flitted in and out of the room at intervals during the evening; had sometimes retired from the light into obscure corners; and, by more than one person, had been observed stealing into the private passages of the house. It was presumed in general, that the man must be known to Williamson. And in some slight degree, as an occasional customer of the house, it is not impossible that he *was*. But afterwards, this repulsive stranger, with his cadaverous ghastliness, extraordinary hair, and glazed eyes, showing himself intermittingly through the hours from 8 to 11 P.M., revolved upon the memory of all who had steadily observed him with something of the same freezing effect as belongs to the two assassins in 'Macbeth,' who present themselves reeking from the murder of Banquo, and gleaming dimly, with dreadful faces, from the misty background, athwart the pomps of the regal banquet.

Meantime the clock struck eleven; the company broke up; the door of entrance was nearly closed; and at this moment of general dispersion the situation of the five inmates left upon the premises was precisely this: the three elders, viz., Williamson, his wife, and his female servant, were all occupied on the ground floor—Williamson himself was drawing ale, porter, &c., for those neighbors, in whose favor the house-door had been left ajar, until the hour of twelve should strike; Mrs. Williamson and her servant were moving to and fro between the back-kitchen and a little parlor; the little grand-daughter, whose sleeping-room was on the *first* floor (which term in London means always the floor raised by one flight of stairs above the level of the street), had been fast asleep since nine o'clock; lastly, the journeyman artisan had retired to rest for some time. He was a regular lodger in the house; and his bedroom was on the second floor. For some time he had been undressed, and had lain down in bed. Being, as a working man, bound to habits of early rising, he was naturally anxious to fall asleep as soon as possible. But, on this particular night, his uneasiness, arising from the recent murders at No. 29, rose to a paroxysm of nervous excitement which kept him awake. It is possible, that from somebody he had heard of the suspicious-looking stranger, or might even personally observed him slinking about. But, were it otherwise, he was aware of several circumstances dangerously affecting this house; for instance, the ruffianism of this whole neighborhood, and the disagreeable fact that the Marrs had lived within a few doors of this very house, which again argued that the murderer also lived at no great distance. These were matters of *general* alarm. But there were others peculiar to this house; in particular, the notoriety of Williamson's opulence; the belief, whether well or ill founded, that he accumulated, in desks and drawers, the money continually flowing into his hands; and lastly, the danger so ostentatiously courted by that habit of leaving the house-door ajar through one entire hour—and that hour loaded with extra danger, by the well-advertised assurance that no collision need be feared with chance convivial visiters, since all such people were banished at eleven. A regulation, which had hitherto operated beneficially for the character and comfort of the house, now, on the contrary, under altered circumstances, became a positive proclamation of exposure and defencelessness, through one entire period of an hour. Williamson himself, it was said generally, being a large un-wieldy man, past seventy, and signally inactive, ought, in prudence, to make the locking of his door coincident with the dismissal of his evening party.

Upon these and other grounds of alarm (par-ticularly this, that Mrs. Williamson was reported to possess a considerable quantity of plate), the journeyman was musing painfully, and the time might be within twenty-eight or twenty-five min-utes of twelve, when all at once, with a crash, pro-claiming some hand of hideous violence, the house-door was suddenly shut and locked. Here, then, beyond all doubt, was the diabolic man, clothed in mystery, from No. 29 Ratcliffe High-way. Yes, that dreadful being, who for twelve days had employed all thoughts and all tongues, was now, too certainly, in this defenceless house, and would, in a few minutes, be face to face with every one of its inmates. A question still lingered in the public mind—whether at Marr's there might not have been *two* men at work. If so, there would be two at present; and one of the two would be immediately disposable for the up-stairs work; since no danger could obviously be more immediately fatal to such an attack than any alarm given from an upper window to the passengers in the street. Through one half-minute the poor panic-stricken man sat up motionless in bed. But then he rose, his first movement being towards the door of his room. Not for any purpose of securing it against intrusion—too well he knew that there was no fastening of any sort—neither lock, nor bolt; nor was there any such moveable furniture in the room as might have availed to barricade the door, even if time could be counted on for such an attempt. It was no effect of prudence, merely the fascination of killing fear it was, that drove him to open the door. One step brought him to the head of the stairs: he lowered his head over the balustrade in order to listen; and at that moment ascended, from the little parlor, this agonizing cry from the woman-servant, 'Lord Jesus Christ! we shall all be murdered!' What a Medusa's head must have lurked in those dreadful bloodless features, and those glazed rigid eyes, that seemed rightfully belonging to a

corpse, when one glance at them sufficed to pro-
claim a death-warrant.

Three separate death-struggles were by this
time over; and the poor petrified journeyman,
quite unconscious of what he was doing, in blind,
passive, self-surrender to panic, absolutely descended both flights of stairs. Infinite terror inspired him with the same impulse as might have
been inspired by headlong courage. In his shirt,
and upon old decaying stairs, that at times
creaked under his feet, he continued to descend,
until he had reached the lowest step but four. The
situation was tremendous beyond any that is on
record. A sneeze, a cough, almost a breathing, and
the young man would be a corpse, without a
chance or a struggle for his life. The murderer was
at that time in the little parlor —the door of which
parlor faced you in descending the stairs; and this
door stood ajar; indeed, much more considerably
open than what is understood by the term 'ajar.'
Of that quadrant, or 90 degrees, which the door
would describe in swinging so far open as to
stand at right angles to the lobby, or to itself, in a
closed position, 55 degrees at the least were exposed. Consequently, two out of three corpses
were exposed to the young man's gaze. Where
was the third? And the murderer—where was he?
As to the murderer, he was walking rapidly backwards and forwards in the parlor, audible but not
visible at first, being engaged with something or

other in that part of the room which the door still concealed. What the something might be, the sound soon explained; he was applying keys tentatively to a cupboard, a closet, and a scrutoire, in the hidden part of the room. Very soon, however, he came into view; but, fortunately for the young man, at this critical moment, the murderer's purpose too entirely absorbed him to allow of his throwing a glance to the staircase, on which else the white figure of the journeyman, standing in motionless horror, would have been detected in one instant, and seasoned for the grave in the second. As to the third corpse, the missing corpse, viz., Mr. Williamson's, *that* is in the cellar; and how its local position can be accounted for, remains a separate question much discussed at the time, but never satisfactorily cleared up. Meantime, that Williamson was dead, became evident to the young man; since else he would have been heard stirring or groaning. Three friends, therefore, out of four, whom the young man had parted with forty minutes ago, were now extinguished; remained, therefore, 40 per cent. (a large per centage for Williams to leave); remained, in fact, himself and his pretty young friend, the little granddaughter, whose childish innocence was still slumbering without fear for herself, or grief for her aged grand-parents. If *they* are gone for ever, happily one friend (for such he will prove himself, indeed, if from such a danger he can save this child) is pretty near to her. But alas! he is still nearer to a murderer. At this moment he is unnerved for any exertion whatever; he has changed into a pillar of ice; for the objects before him, separated by just thirteen feet, are these:—The housemaid had been caught by the murderer on her knees; she was kneeling before the fire-grate, which she had been polishing with black lead. That part of her task was finished; and she had passed on to another task, viz., the filling of the grate with wood and coals, not for kindling at this moment, but so as to have it ready for kindling on the next day. The appearances all showed that she must have been engaged in this labor at the very moment when the murderer entered; and perhaps the succession of the incidents arranged itself as follows:—From the awful ejaculation and loud outcry to Christ, as overheard by the journeyman, it was clear that then first she had been alarmed; yet this was at least one and a-half or even two minutes after the door-slamming. Consequently the alarm which had so fearfully and seasonably alarmed the young man, must, in some unaccountable way, have been misinterpreted by the two women. It was said, at the time, that Mrs. Williamson labored under some dulness of hearing; and it was conjectured that the servant, having her ears filled with the noise of her own scrubbing, and her head half under the grate, might have confounded it with the street noises, or else might have imputed this violent closure to some mischievous boys. But, howsoever explained, the fact was evident, that, until the words of appeal to Christ, the servant had noticed nothing suspicious, nothing which interrupted her labors. If so, it followed that neither had Mrs. Williamson noticed anything; for, in that case, she would have communicated her own alarm to the servant, since both were in the same small room. Apparently the course of things after the murderer had entered the room was this:—Mrs. Williamson had probably not seen him, from the accident of standing with her back to the door. Her, therefore, before he was himself observed at all, he had stunned and prostrated by a shattering blow on the back of her head; this blow, inflicted by a crow-bar, had smashed in the hinder part of the skull. She fell; and by the noise of her fall (for all was the work of a moment) had first roused the attention of the servant; who then uttered the cry which had reached the young man; but before she could repeat it, the murderer had descended with his uplifted instrument upon *her* head, crushing the skull inwards upon the brain. Both the women were irrecoverably destroyed, so that further outrages were needless; and, moreover, the murderer was conscious of the imminent danger from delay; and yet, in spite of his hurry, so fully did he appreciate the fatal consequences to himself, if any of his victims should so far revive into consciousness as to make circumstantial depositions, that, by way of making this impossible, he had proceeded instantly to cut the throats of each. All this tallied with the appearances as now presenting themselves. Mrs. Williamson had fallen backwards with her head to the door; the servant, from her kneeling posture, had been incapable of rising, and had presented her head passively to blows; after which, the miscreant had but to bend her head backwards so as to expose her throat, and the murder was finished.

It is remarkable that the young artisan, paralyzed as he had been by fear, and evidently fascinated for a time so as to walk right towards the lion's mouth, yet found himself able to notice everything important. The reader must suppose him at this point watching the murderer whilst hanging over the body of Mrs. Williamson, and whilst renewing his search for certain important keys. Doubtless it was an anxious situation for the murderer; for, unless he speedily found the keys wanted, all this hideous tragedy would end in nothing but a prodigious increase of the public horror, in tenfold precautions therefore, and redoubled obstacles interposed between himself and his future game. Nay, there was even a nearer interest at stake; his own immediate safety might, by a probable accident, be compromised. Most of those who came to the house for liquor were giddy girls or children, who, on finding this house closed, would go off carelessly to some other; but, let any thoughtful woman or man come to the door now, a full quarter of an hour before the established time of closing, in that case suspicion would arise too powerful to be checked. There would be a sudden alarm given; after which, mere luck would decide the event. For it is a remarkable fact, and one that illustrates the singular inconsistency of this villain, who, being often so superfluously subtle, was in other directions so reckless and improvident, that at this very moment, standing amongst corpses that had deluged the little parlor with blood, Williams must have been in considerable doubt whether he had any sure means of egress. There were windows, he knew, to the back; but upon what ground they opened, he seems to have had no certain information; and in a neighborhood so dangerous, the windows of the lower story would not improbably be nailed down; those in the upper might be free, but then came the necessity of a leap too formidable. From all this, however, the sole practical inference was to hurry forward with the trial of further keys, and to detect the hidden treasure. This it was, this intense absorption in one overmastering pursuit, that dulled the murderer's perceptions as to all around him; otherwise, he must have heard the breathing of the young man, which to himself at times became fearfully audible. As the murderer stood once more over the body of Mrs. Williamson, and searched her pockets more narrowly, he pulled out various clusters of keys, one of which dropping, gave a harsh gingling sound upon the floor. At this time it was that the secret witness, from his secret stand, noticed the fact of Williams's surtout being lined with silk of the finest quality. One other fact he noticed, which eventually became more immediately important than many stronger circumstances of incrimination; this was, that the shoes of the murderer, apparently new, and bought, probably, with poor Marr's money, creaked as he walked, harshly and frequently. With the new clusters of keys, the murderer walked off to the hidden section of the parlor. And here, at last, was suggested to the journeyman the sudden opening for an escape. Some minutes would be lost to a certainty trying all these keys; and subsequently in searching the drawers, supposing that the keys answered—or in violently forcing them, supposing that they did *not*. He might thus count upon a brief interval of leisure, whilst the rattling of the keys might obscure to the murderer the creaking of the stairs under the re-ascending journeyman. His plan was now formed: on regaining his bedroom, he placed the bed against the door by way of a transient retardation to the enemy, that might give him a short warning, and in the worst extremity, might give him a chance for life by means of a desperate leap. This change made

as quietly as possible, he tore the sheets, pillow-
cases, and blankets into broad ribbons; and after
plaiting them into ropes, spliced the different
lengths together. But at the very first he descries
this ugly addition to his labors. Where shall he
look for any staple, hook, bar, or other fixture,
from which his rope, when twisted, may safely
depend? Measured from the window-*sill—i.e.*, the
lowest part of the window architrave—there
count but twenty-two or twenty-three feet to the
ground. Of this length ten or twelve feet may be
looked upon as cancelled, because to that extent
he might drop without danger. So much being de-
ducted, there would remain, say, a dozen feet of
rope to prepare. But, unhappily, there is no stout
iron fixture anywhere about his window. The
nearest, indeed the sole fixture of that sort, is not
near to the window at all; it is a spike fixed (for no
reason at all that is apparent) in the bed-tester;
now, the bed being shifted, the spike is shifted;
and its distance from the window, having been always four feet, is now seven. Seven entire feet,
therefore, must be added to that which would
have sufficed if measured from the window. But
courage! God, by the proverb of all nations in
Christendom, helps those that help themselves.
This our young man thankfully acknowledges; he
reads already, in the very fact of any spike at all
being found where hitherto it has been useless, an
earnest of providential aid. Were it only for him-

self that he worked, he could not feel himself meritoriously employed; but this is not so; in deep
sincerity, he is now agitated for the poor child,
whom he knows and loves; every minute, he feels,
brings ruin nearer to *her*; and, as he passed her
door, his first thought had been to take her out of
bed in his arms, and to carry her where she might
share his chances. But, on consideration, he felt
that this sudden awaking of her, and the impossibility of even whispering any explanation, would
cause her to cry audibly; and the inevitable indiscretion of one would be fatal to the two. As the
Alpine avalanches, when suspended above the
traveller's head, oftentimes (we are told) come
down through the stirring of the air by a simple
whisper, precisely on such a tenure of a whisper
was now suspended the murderous malice of the
man below. No; there is but one way to save the
child; towards *her* deliverance, the first step is
through his own. And he has made an excellent
beginning; for the spike, which too fearfully he
had expected to see torn away by any strain upon
the half-carious wood, stands firmly when tried
against the pressure of his own weight. He has
rapidly fastened on to it three lengths of his new
rope, measuring eleven feet. He plaits it roughly;
so that only three feet have been lost in the intertwisting; he has spliced on a second length equal
to the first; so that, already, sixteen feet are ready
to throw out of the window; and thus, let the

worst come to the worst, it will not be absolute ruin to swarm down the rope so far as it will reach, and then to drop boldly. All this has been accomplished in about six minutes; and the hot contest between above and below is steadily but fervently proceeding. Murderer is working hard in the parlor; journeyman is working hard in the bedroom. Miscreant is getting on famously down-stairs; one batch of bank-notes he has already bagged; and is hard upon the scent of a second. He has also sprung a covey of golden coins. Sovereigns as yet were not; but guineas at this period fetched thirty shillings a-piece; and he has worked his way into a little quarry of these. Murderer is almost joyous; and if any creature is still living in this house, as shrewdly he suspects, and very soon means to know, with that creature he would be happy, before cutting the creature's throat, to drink a glass of something. Instead of the glass, might he not make a present to the poor creature of its throat? Oh no! impossible! Throats are a sort of thing that he never makes presents of; business — business must be attended to. Really the two men, considered simply as men of business, are both meritorious. Like chorus and semi-chorus, strophe and antistrophe, they work each against the other. Pull journeyman, pull murderer! Pull baker, pull devil! As regards the journeyman, he is now safe. To his sixteen feet, of which seven are neutralized by the distance of the bed, he has at last added six feet more, which will be short of reaching the ground by perhaps ten feet—a trifle which man or boy may drop without injury. All is safe, therefore, for him: which is more than one can be sure of for miscreant in the parlor. Miscreant, however, takes it coolly enough: the reason being, that, with all his cleverness, for once in his life miscreant has been over-reached. The reader and I know, but miscreant does not in the least suspect, a little fact of some importance, viz., that just now through a space of full three minutes he has been overlooked and studied by one, who (though reading in a dreadful book, and suffering under mortal panic) took accurate notes of so much as his limited opportunities allowed him to see, and will assuredly report the creaking shoes and the silk-mounted surtout in quarters where such little facts will tell very little to his advantage. But, although it is true that Mr. Williams, unaware of the journeyman's having 'assisted' at the examination of Mrs. Williamson's pockets, could not connect any anxiety with that person's subsequent proceedings', nor specially, therefore, with his having embarked in the rope-weaving line, assuredly he knew of reasons enough for not loitering. And yet he *did* loiter. Reading his acts by the light of such mute traces as he left behind him, the police became aware that latterly he must have loitered. And the reason which governed him is striking; because at once it records—that murder was not pursued by him simply as a means to an end, but also as an end for itself. Mr. Williams had now been upon the premises for perhaps fifteen or twenty minutes; and in that space of time he had dispatched, in a style satisfactory to himself, a considerable amount of business. He had done, in commercial language, 'a good stroke of business.' Upon two floors, viz., the cellar-floor and the ground-floor, he has 'accounted for' all the population. But there remained at least two floors more; and it now occurred to Mr. Williams that, although the landlord's somewhat chilling manner had shut him out from any familiar knowledge of the household arrangements, too probably on one or other of those floors there must be some throats. As to plunder, he has already bagged the whole. And it was next to impossible that any arrear the most trivial should still remain for a gleaner. But the throats—the throats—there it was that arrears and gleanings might perhaps be counted on. And thus it appeared that, in his wolfish thirst for blood, Mr. Williams put to hazard the whole fruits of his night's work, and his life into the bargain. At this moment, if the murderer knew all, could he see the open window above stairs ready for the descent of the journeyman, could he witness the life-and-death rapidity with which that journeyman is working, could he guess at the almighty uproar which within ninety seconds will be maddening the population of this populous district—no picture of a maniac in flight of panic or in pursuit of vengeance would adequately represent the agony of haste with which he would himself be hurrying to the street-door for final evasion. That mode of escape was still free. Even at this moment, there yet remained time sufficient for a successful flight, and, therefore, for the following revolution in the romance of his own abominable life. He had in his pockets above a hundred pounds of booty; means, therefore, for a full disguise. This very night, if he will shave off his yellow hair, and blacken his eyebrows, buying, when morning light returns, a dark-colored wig, and clothes such as may co-operate in personating the character of a grave professional man, he may elude all suspicions of impertinent policemen; may sail by any one of a hundred vessels bound for any port along the huge line of sea-board (stretching through twenty-four hundred miles) of the American United States; may enjoy fifty years for leisurely repentance; and may even die in the odor of sanctity. On the other hand, if he prefer active life, it is not impossible that, with *his* subtlety, hardihood, and unscrupulousness, in a land where the simple process of naturalization converts the alien at once into a child of the family, he might rise to the president's chair; might have a statue at his death; and afterwards a life in three volumes quarto, with no hint glancing towards No. 29 Ratcliffe Highway.

But all depends on the next ninety seconds. Within that time there is a sharp turn to be taken; there is a wrong turn, and a right turn. Should his better angel guide him to the right one, all may yet go well as regards this world's prosperity. But behold! in two minutes from this point we shall see him take the wrong one: and then Nemesis will be at his heels with ruin perfect and sudden.

Meantime, if the murderer allows himself to loiter, the ropemaker overhead does *not*. Well he knows that the poor child's fate is on the edge of a razor: for all turns upon the alarm being raised before the murderer reaches her bedside. And at this very moment, whilst desperate agitation is nearly paralyzing his fingers, he hears the sullen stealthy step of the murderer creeping up through the darkness. It had been the expectation of the journeyman (founded on the clamorous uproar with which the street-door was slammed) that Williams, when disposable for his up-stairs work, would come racing at a long jubilant gallop, and with a tiger roar; and perhaps, on his natural instincts, he would have done so. But this mode of approach, which was of dreadful effect when applied to a case of surprise, became dangerous in the case of people who might by this time have been placed fully upon their guard. The step which he had heard was on the staircase—but upon which stair? He fancied upon the lowest: and in a movement so slow and cautious, even this might make all the difference; yet might it not have been the tenth, twelfth, or fourteenth stair? Never, perhaps, in this world did any man feel his own responsibility so cruelly loaded and strained, as at this moment did the poor journeyman on behalf of the slumbering child. Lose but two seconds, through awkwardness or through the self-counteractions of panic, and for *her* the total difference arose between life and death. Still there is a hope: and nothing can so frightfully expound the hellish nature of him whose baleful shadow, to speak astrologically, at this moment darkens the house of life, than the simple expression of the ground on which this hope rested. The journeyman felt sure that the murderer would not be satisfied to kill the poor child whilst unconscious. This would be to defeat his whole purpose in murdering her at all. To an epicure in murder such as Williams, it would be taking away the very sting of the enjoyment, if the poor child should be suffered to drink off the bitter cup of death without fully apprehending the misery of the situation. But this luckily would require time: the double confusion of mind, first, from being roused up at so unusual an hour, and, secondly, from the horror of the occasion when explained to her, would at first produce fainting, or some mode of insensibility or distraction, such as must occupy a considerable time. The logic of the case, in short, all rested upon the *ultra* fiendishness of Williams.

Were he likely to be content with the mere fact of the child's death, apart from the process and leisurely expansion of its mental agony—in that case there would be no hope. But, because our present murderer is fastidiously finical in his exactions—a sort of martinet in the scenical grouping and draping of the circumstances in his murders —therefore it is that hope becomes reasonable, since all such refinements of preparation demand time. Murders of mere necessity Williams was obliged to hurry; but, in a murder of pure voluptuousness, entirely disinterested, where no hostile witness was to be removed, no extra booty to be gained, and no revenge to be gratified, it is clear that to hurry would be altogether to ruin. If this child, therefore, is to be saved, it will be on pure aesthetical considerations. [4]

But all considerations whatever are at this moment suddenly cut short. A second step is heard on the stairs, but still stealthy and cautious; a third —and then the child's doom seems fixed. But just at that. moment all is ready. The window is wide open; the rope is swinging free; the journeyman has launched himself; and already he is in the first stage of his descent. Simply by the weight of his person he descended, and by the resistance of his hands he retarded the descent. The danger was, that the rope should run too smoothly through his hands, and that by too rapid an acceleration of pace he should come violently to the ground.

Happily he was able to resist the descending impetus: the knots of the splicings furnished a succession of retardations. But the rope proved shorter by four or five feet than he had calculated: ten or eleven feet from the ground he hung suspended in the air; speechless for the present, through long-continued agitation; and not daring to drop boldly on the rough carriage pavement, lest he should fracture his legs. But the night was not dark, as it had been on occasion of the Marr murders. And yet, for purposes of criminal police, it was by accident worse than the darkest night that ever hid a murder or baffled a pursuit. London, from east to west, was covered with a deep pall (rising from the river) of universal fog. Hence it happened, that for twenty or thirty seconds the young man hanging in the air was not observed. His white shirt at length attracted notice. Three or four people ran up, and received him in their arms, all anticipating some dreadful annunciation. To what house did he belong? Even *that* was not instantly apparent; but he pointed with his finger to Williamson's door, and said in a half-choking whisper—'*Marr's murderer, now at work!*'

All explained itself in a moment: the silent language of the fact made its own eloquent revelation. The mysterious exterminator of No. 29 Ratcliffe Highway had visited another house; and, behold! one man only had escaped through the air, and in his night-dress, to tell the tale. Superstitiously, there was something to check the pursuit of this unintelligible criminal. Morally, and in the interests of vindictive justice, there was everything to rouse, quicken, and sustain it.

Yes, Marr's murderer—the man of mystery—was again at work; at this moment perhaps extinguishing some lamp of life, and not at any remote place, but here—in the very house which the listeners to this dreadful announcement were actually touching. The chaos and blind uproar of the scene which followed, measured by the crowded reports in the journals of many subsequent days, and in one feature of that case, has never to my knowledge had its parallel; or, if a parallel, only in one case—what followed, I mean, on the acquittal of the seven bishops at Westminster in 1688. At present there was more than passionate enthusiasm. The frenzied movement of mixed horror and exultation—the ululation of vengeance which ascended instantaneously from the individual street, and then by a sublime sort of magnetic contagion from all the adjacent streets, can be adequately expressed only by a rapturous passage in Shelley:—

> 'The transport of a fierce and
> monstrous gladness
> Spread through the multi-
> tudinous streets, fast
> flying

Upon the wings of fear:—
  From his dull madness
  The starveling waked, and
  died in joy: the dying,
Among the corpses in stark
  agony lying,
  Just heard the happy tid-
  ings, and in hope
Closed their faint eyes: from
  house to house replying
  With loud acclaim the
  living shook heaven's
  cope,
And fill'd the startled earth
  with echoes.'[5]

There was something, indeed, half inexplicable in the instantaneous interpretation of the gathering shout according to its true meaning. In fact, the deadly roar of vengeance, and its sublime unity, *could* point in this district only to the one demon whose idea had brooded and tyrannized, for twelve days, over the general heart: every door, every window in the neighborhood, flew open as if at a word of command; multitudes, without waiting for the regular means of egress, leaped down at once from the windows on the lower story; sick men rose from their beds; in one instance, as if expressly to verify the image of Shelley (in v. 4, 5, 6, 7), a man whose death had been looked for through some days, and who actually *did* die on the following day, rose, armed himself with a sword, and descended in his shirt into the street. The chance was a good one, and the mob were made aware of it, for catching the wolfish dog in the high noon and carnival of his bloody revels—in the very centre of his own shambles. For a moment the mob was self-baffled by its own numbers and its own fury. But even that fury felt the call for self-control. It was evident that the massy street-door must be driven in, since there was no longer any living person to co-operate with their efforts from within, excepting only a female child. Crowbars dexterously applied in one minute threw the door out of hangings, and the people entered like a torrent. It may be guessed with what fret and irritation to their consuming fury, a signal of pause and absolute silence was made by a person of local importance. In the hope of receiving some useful communication, the mob became silent. 'Now listen,' said the man of authority, 'and we shall learn whether he is above-stairs or below.' Immediately a noise was heard as if of some one forcing windows, and clearly the sound came from a bedroom above. Yes, the fact was apparent that the murderer was even yet in the house: he had been caught in a trap. Not having made himself familiar with the details of Williamson's house, to all appearance he had suddenly become a prisoner in one of the upper rooms. Towards this the crowd now rushed impetuously. The door, however, was found to be slightly fastened; and, at the moment when this was forced, a loud crash of the window, both glass and frame, announced that the wretch had made his escape. He had leaped down; and several persons in the crowd, who burned with the general fury, leaped after him. These persons had not troubled themselves about the nature of the ground; but now, on making an examination of it with torches, they reported it to be an inclined plane, or embankment of clay, very wet and adhesive. The prints of the man's footsteps were deeply impressed upon the clay, and therefore easily traced up to the summit of the embankment; but it was perceived at once that pursuit would be useless, from the density of the mist. Two feet ahead of you, a man was entirely withdrawn from your power of identification; and, on overtaking him, you could not venture to challenge him as the same whom you had lost sight of. Never, through the course of a whole century, could there be a night expected more propitious to an escaping criminal: means of disguise Williams now had in excess; and the dens were innumerable in the neighborhood of the river that could have sheltered him for years from troublesome inquiries. But favors are thrown away upon the reckless and the thankless. That night, when the turning-point offered itself for his whole future career, Williams took the wrong turn; for, out of mere indolence, he took the turn to his old lodgings—that place which, in all England, he had just now the most reason to shun.

Meantime the crowd had thoroughly searched the premises of Williamson. The first inquiry was for the young grand-daughter. Williams, it was evident, had gone into her room: but in this room apparently it was that the sudden uproar in the streets had surprised him; after which his undivided attention had been directed to the windows, since through these only any retreat had been left open to him. Even this retreat he owed only to the fog and to the hurry of the moment, and to the difficulty of approaching the premises by the rear. The little girl was naturally agitated by the influx of strangers at that hour; but otherwise, through the humane precautions of the neighbors, she was preserved from all knowledge of the dreadful events that had occurred whilst she herself was sleeping. Her poor old grandfather was still missing, until the crowd descended into the cellar; he was then found lying prostrate on the cellar floor: apparently he had been thrown down from the top of the cellar stairs, and with so much violence, that one leg was broken. After he had been thus disabled, Williams had gone down to him, and cut his throat. There was much discussion at the time, in some of the public journals, upon the possibility of reconciling these incidents with other circumstantialities of the case, supposing that only one man had been concerned in the affair. That there *was* only one man concerned, seems to be certain. One only was seen or heard at Marr's: one only, and beyond all doubt the same man, was seen by the young journeyman in Mrs. Williamson's parlor; and one only was traced by his footmarks on the clay embankment. Apparently the course which he had pursued was this: he had introduced himself to Williamson by ordering some beer. This order would oblige the old man to go down into the cellar; Williams would wait until he had reached it, and would then 'slam' and lock the street-door in the violent way described. Williamson would come up in agitation upon hearing this violence. The murderer, aware that he would do so, met him, no doubt, at the head of the cellar stairs, and threw him down; after which he would go down to consummate the murder in his ordinary way. All this would occupy a minute, or a minute and a half; and in that way the interval would be accounted for that elapsed between the alarming sound of the street-door as heard by the journeyman, and the lamentable outcry of the female servant. It is evident also, that the reason why no cry whatsoever had been heard from the lips of Mrs. Williamson, is due to the positions of the parties as I have sketched them. Coming behind Mrs. Williamson, unseen therefore, and from her deafness unheard, the murderer would inflict entire abolition of consciousness while she was yet unaware of his presence. But with the servant, who had unavoidably witnessed the attack upon her mistress, the murderer could not obtain the same fulness of advantage; and *she* therefore had time for making an agonizing ejaculation.

It has been mentioned, that the murderer of the Marrs was not for nearly a fortnight so much as suspected; meaning that, previously to the Williamson murder, no vestige of any ground for suspicion in any direction whatever had occurred either to the general public or to the police. But there were two very limited exceptions to this state of absolute ignorance. Some of the magistrates had in their possession something which, when closely examined, offered a very probable means for tracing the criminal. But as yet they had *not* traced him. Until the Friday morning next after the destruction of the Williamsons, they had not published the important fact, that upon the ship-carpenter's mallet (with which, as regarded the stunning or disabling process, the murders had been achieved) were inscribed the letters 'J. P.' This mallet had, by a strange oversight on the part of the murderer, been left behind in Marr's shop; and it is an interesting fact, therefore, that, had the villain been intercepted by the brave pawnbroker, he would have been met virtually disarmed. This public notification was made officially on the Fri-

day, viz., on the thirteenth day after the first murder. And it was instantly followed (as will be
seen) by a most important result. Meantime,
within the secrecy of one single bedroom in all
London, it is a fact that Williams had been whisperingly the object of very deep suspicion from
the very first—that is, within that same hour
which witnessed the Marr tragedy. And singular
it is, that the suspicion was due entirely to his
own folly. Williams lodged, in company with
other men of various nations, at a public-house. In
a large dormitory there were arranged five or six
beds; these were occupied by artisans, generally
of respectable character. One or two Englishmen
there were, one or two Scotchmen, three or four
Germans, and Williams, whose birth-place was
not certainly known. On the fatal Saturday night,
about half-past one o'clock, when Williams returned from his dreadful labors, he found the
English and Scotch party asleep, but the Germans
awake: one of them was sitting up with a lighted
candle in his hands, and reading aloud to the
other two. Upon this, Williams said, in an angry
and very peremptory tone, 'Oh, put that candle
out; put it out directly; we shall all be burned in
our beds.' Had the British party in the room been
awake, Mr. Williams would have roused a muti-
nous protest against this arrogant mandate. But
Germans are generally mild and facile in their
tempers; so the light was complaisantly extin-

guished. Yet, as there were no curtains, it struck the Germans that the danger was really none at all; for bed-clothes, massed upon each other, will no more burn than the leaves of a closed book. Privately, therefore, the Germans drew an inference, that Mr. Williams must have had some urgent motive for withdrawing his own person and dress from observation. What this motive might be, the next day's news diffused all over London, and of course at this house, not two furlongs from Marr's shop, made awfully evident; and, as may well be supposed, the suspicion was communicated to the other members of the dormitory. All of them, however, were aware of the legal danger attaching, under English law, to insinuations against a man, even if true, which might not admit of proof. In reality, had Williams used the most obvious precautions, had he simply walked down to the Thames (not a stone's-throw distant), and flung two of his implements into the river, no conclusive proof could have been adduced against him. And he might have realized the scheme of Courvoisier (the murderer of Lord William Russell) —viz., have sought each separate month's support in a separate well- concerted murder. The party in the dormitory, meantime, were satisfied themselves, but waited for evidences that might satisfy others. No sooner, therefore, had the official notice been published as to the initials J. P. on the mallet, than every man in the house recognized at once the well- known initials of an honest Norwegian ship-carpenter, John Petersen, who had worked in the English dockyards until the present year; but, having occasion to revisit his native land, had left his box of tools in the garrets of this inn. These garrets were now searched. Petersen's tool- chest was found, but wanting the mallet; and, on further examination, another overwhelming discovery was made. The surgeon, who examined the corpses at Williamson's, had given it as his opinion that the throats were not cut by means of a razor, but of some implement differently shaped. It was now remembered that Williams had recently borrowed a large French knife of peculiar construction; and accordingly, from a heap of old lumber and rags, there was soon extricated a waistcoat, which the whole house could swear to as recently worn by Williams. In this waistcoat, and glued by gore to the lining of its pockets, was found the French knife. Next, it was matter of notoriety to everybody in the inn, that Williams ordinarily wore at present a pair of creaking shoes, and a brown surtout lined with silk. Many other presumptions seemed scarcely called for. Williams was immediately apprehended, and briefly examined. This was on the Friday. On the Saturday morning (viz., fourteen days from the Marr murders) he was again brought up. The circumstantial evidence was overwhelming; Williams watched its course, but said very little. At the close, he was fully committed for trial at the next sessions; and it is needless to say, that, on his road to prison, he was pursued by mobs so fierce, that, under ordinary circumstances, there would have been small hope of escaping summary vengeance. But upon this occasion a powerful escort had been provided; so that he was safely lodged in jail. In this particular jail at this time, the regulation was, that at five o'clock, P. M. all the prisoners on the criminal side should be finally locked up for the night, and without candles. For fourteen hours (that is, until seven o'clock on the next morning) they were left unvisited, and in total darkness. Time, therefore, Williams had for committing suicide. The means in other respects were small. One iron bar there was, meant (if I remember) for the suspension of a lamp; upon this he had hanged himself by his braces. At what hour was uncertain: some people fancied at midnight. And in that case, precisely at the hour when, fourteen days before, he had been spreading horror and desolation through the quiet family of poor Marr, now was he forced into drinking of the same cup, presented to his lips by the same accursed hands.

~

The case of the M'Keans, which has been specially alluded to, merits also a slight rehearsal for the dreadful picturesqueness of some two or three amongst its circumstances. The scene of this murder was at a rustic inn, some few miles (I think) from Manchester; and the advantageous situation of this inn it was, out of which arose the two fold temptations of the case. Generally speaking, an inn argues, of course, a close cincture of neighbors—as the original motive for opening such an establishment. But, in this case, the house individually was solitary, so that no interruption was to be looked for from any persons living within reach of screams; and yet, on the other hand, the circumjacent vicinity was eminently populous; as one consequence of which, a benefit club had established its weekly rendezvous in this inn, and left the peculiar accumulations in their club- room, under the custody of the landlord. This fund arose often to a considerable amount, fifty or seventy pounds, before it was transferred to the hands of a banker. Here, therefore, was a treasure worth some little risk, and a situation that promised next to none. These attractive circumstances had, by accident, become accurately known to one or both of the two M'Keans; and, unfortunately, at a moment of overwhelming misfortune to themselves. They were hawkers; and, until lately, had borne most respectable characters: but some mercantile crash had overtaken them with utter ruin, in which their joint capital had been swallowed up to the last shilling. This sudden prostration had made them desperate: their own little property had been swallowed up in a large *social* catastrophe, and society at large they looked upon as accountable to them for a robbery. In preying, therefore, upon society, they considered themselves as pursuing a wild natural justice of retaliation. The money aimed at did certainly assume the character of public money, being the product of many separate subscriptions. They forgot, however, that in the murderous acts, which too certainly they meditated as preliminaries to the robbery, they could plead no such imaginary social precedent. In dealing with a family that seemed almost helpless, if all went smoothly, they relied entirely upon their own bodily strength. They were stout young men, twenty-eight to thirty-two years old; somewhat undersized as to height; but squarely built, deep-chested, broad-shouldered, and so beautifully formed, as regarded the symmetry of their limbs and their articulations, that, after their execution, the bodies were privately exhibited by the surgeons of the Manchester Infirmary, as objects of statuesque interest. On the other hand, the household which they proposed to attack consisted of the following four persons:—1. the landlord, a stoutish farmer—but *him* they intended to disable by a trick then newly introduced amongst robbers, and termed *hocussing, i.e.,* clandestinely drugging the liquor of the victim with laudanum;

2. the landlord's wife; 3. a young servant woman; 4. a boy, twelve or fourteen years old. The danger was, that out of four persons, scattered by possibility over a house which had two separate exits, one at least might escape, and by better acquaintance with the adjacent paths, might succeed in giving an alarm to some of the houses a furlong distant. Their final resolution was, to be guided by circumstances as to the mode of conducting the affair; and yet, as it seemed essential to success that they should assume the air of strangers to each other, it was necessary that they should pre-concert some general outline of their plan; since it would on this scheme be impossible, without awaking violent suspicions, to make any communications under the eyes of the family. This outline included, at the least, one murder: so much was settled; but, otherwise, their subsequent proceedings make it evident that they wished to have as little bloodshed as was consistent with their final object. On the appointed day, they presented themselves separately at the rustic inn, and at different hours. One came as early as four o'clock in the afternoon; the other not until half-past seven. They saluted each other distantly and shyly; and, though occasionally exchanging a few words in the character of strangers, did not seem disposed to any familiar intercourse. With the landlord, however, on his return about eight o'clock from Manchester, one of the brothers entered into a

lively conversation; invited him to take a tumbler of punch; and, at a moment when the landlord's absence from the room allowed it, poured into the punch a spoonful of laudanum. Some time after this, the clock struck ten; upon which the elder M'Kean, professing to be weary, asked to be shown up to his bedroom: for each brother, immediately on arriving, had engaged a bed. On this, the poor servant girl had presented herself with a bed-candle to light him upstairs. At this critical moment the family were distributed thus:—the landlord, stupefied with the horrid narcotic which he had drunk, had retired to a private room adjoining the public room, for the purpose of reclining upon a sofa: and he, luckily for his own safety, was looked upon as entirely incapacitated for action. The landlady was occupied with her husband. And thus the younger M'Kean was left alone in the public room. He rose, therefore, softly, and placed himself at the foot of the stairs which his brother had just ascended, so as to be sure of intercepting any fugitive from the bedroom above. Into that room the elder M'Kean was ushered by the servant, who pointed to two beds—one of which was already half occupied by the boy, and the other empty: in these, she intimated that the two strangers must dispose of themselves for the night, according to any arrangement that they might agree upon. Saying this, she presented him with the candle, which he in a moment placed upon the table; and, intercepting her retreat from the room threw his arm round her neck with a gesture as though he meant to kiss her. This was evidently what she herself anticipated, and endeavored to prevent. Her horror may be imagined, when she felt the perfidious hand that clasped her neck armed with a razor, and violently cutting her throat. She was hardly able to utter one scream, before she sank powerless upon the floor. This dreadful spectacle was witnessed by the boy, who was not asleep, but had presence of mind enough instantly to close his eyes. The murderer advanced hastily to the bed, and anxiously examined the expression of the boy's features: satisfied he was not, and he then placed his hand upon the boy's heart, in order to judge by its beatings whether he were agitated or not. This was a dreadful trial: and no doubt the counterfeit sleep would immediately have been detected, when suddenly a dreadful spectacle drew off the attention of the murderer. Solemnly, and in ghostly silence, uprose in her dying delirium the murdered girl; she stood upright, she walked steadily for a moment or two, she bent her steps towards the door. The murderer turned away to pursue her; and at that moment the boy, feeling that his one solitary chance was to fly while this scene was in progress, bounded out of bed. On the landing at the head of the stairs was one murderer, at the foot of the stairs was the other: who could believe that the boy had the shadow of a chance for escaping? And yet, in the most natural way, he surmounted all hindrances. In the boy's horror, he laid his left hand on the balustrade, and took a flying leap over it, which landed him at the bottom of the stairs, without having touched a single stair. He had thus effectually passed one of the murderers: the other, it is true, was still to be passed; and this would have been impossible but for a sudden accident. The landlady had been alarmed by the faint scream of the young woman; had hurried from her private room to the girl's assistance; but at the foot of the stairs had been intercepted by the younger brother, and was at this moment struggling with *him*. The confusion of this life-and- death conflict had allowed the boy to whirl past them. Luckily he took a turn into a kitchen, out of which was a back-door, fastened by a single bolt, that ran freely at a touch; and through this door he rushed into the open fields. But at this moment the elder brother was set free for pursuit by the death of the poor girl. There is no doubt, that in her delirium the image moving through her thoughts was that of the club, which met once a- week. She fancied it no doubt sitting; and to this room, for help and for safety she staggered along; she entered it, and within the doorway once more she dropped down, and instantly expired. Her murderer, who had followed her closely, now saw himself set at liberty for the pursuit of the boy. At this critical moment, all was at stake; unless the boy were caught, the enterprise was ruined. He passed his brother, therefore, and the landlady without pausing, and rushed through the open door into the fields. By a single second, perhaps, he was too late. The boy was keenly aware, that if he continued in sight, he would have no chance of escaping from a powerful young man. He made, therefore, at once for a ditch, into which he tumbled headlong. Had the murderer ventured to make a leisurely examination of the nearest ditch, he would easily have found the boy—made so conspicuous by his white shirt. But he lost all heart, upon failing at once to arrest the boy's flight. And every succeeding second made his despair the greater. If the boy had really effected his escape to the neighboring farm-house, a party of men might be gathered within five minutes; and already it might have become difficult for himself and his brother, unacquainted with the field paths, to evade being intercepted. Nothing remained, therefore, but to summon his brother away. Thus it happened that the landlady, though mangled, escaped with life, and eventually recovered. The landlord owed his safety to the stupefying potion. And the baffled murderers had the misery of knowing that their dreadful crime had been altogether profitless. The road, indeed, was now open to the club-room; and, probably, forty seconds would have sufficed to carry off the box of treasure, which afterwards might have been burst open and pillaged at leisure. But the fear of intercepting enemies was too strongly upon them; and they fled rapidly by a road which carried them actually within six feet of the lurking boy. That night they passed through Manchester. When daylight returned, they slept in a thicket twenty miles distant from the scene of their guilty attempt. On the second and third nights, they pursued their march on foot, resting again during the day. About sunrise on the fourth morning, they were entering some village near Kirby Lonsdale, in Westmoreland. They must have designedly quitted the direct line of route; for their object was Ayrshire, of which county they were natives; and the regular road would have led them through Shap, Penrith, Carlisle. Probably they were seeking to elude the persecution of the stage-coaches, which, for the last thirty hours, had been scattering at all the inns and road-side *cabarets* hand-bills describing their persons and dress. It happened (perhaps through design) that on this fourth morning they had separated, so as to enter the village ten minutes apart from each other. They were exhausted and footsore. In this condition it was easy to stop them. A blacksmith had silently reconnoitred them, and compared their appearance with the description of the hand-bills. They were then easily overtaken, and separately arrested. Their trial and condemnation speedily followed at Lancaster; and in those days it followed, of course, that they were executed. Otherwise their case fell so far within the sheltering limits of what would *now* be regarded as extenuating circumstances—that, whilst a murder more or less was not to repel them from their object, very evidently they were anxious to economize the bloodshed as much as possible. Immeasurable, therefore, was the interval which divided them from the monster Williams. They perished on the scaffold: Williams, as I have said, by his own hand; and, in obedience to the law as it then stood, he was buried in the centre of a *quadrivium*, or conflux of four roads (in this case four streets), with a stake driven through his heart. And over him drives for ever the uproar of unresting London!

---

1. I am not sure whether Southey held at this time his appointment to the editorship of the 'Edinburgh Annual Register.' If he did, no doubt in the domestic section of that chronicle will be found an excellent account of the whole.
2. An artist told me in this year, 1812, that having accidentally seen a native Devonshire regiment (either volunteers or militia), nine hundred strong, marching past a station at which he had posted himself, he did not observe a dozen men that would not have been described in common parlance as 'good looking.'
3. I do not remember, chronologically, the history of gaslights. But in London, long after Mr. Winsor had shown the value of gas-lighting, and its applicability to street purposes, various districts were prevented, for many years,

from resorting to the new system, in consequence of old contracts with oil-dealers, subsisting through long terms of years.

4. Let the reader, who is disposed to regard as exaggerated or romantic the pure fiendishness imputed to Williams, recollect that, except for the luxurious purpose of basking and revelling in the anguish of dying despair, he had no motive at all, small or great, for attempting the murder of this young girl. She had seen nothing, heard nothing—was fast asleep, and her door was closed; so that, as a witness against him, he knew that she was as useless as any one of the three corpses. And yet he *was* making preparations for her murder, when the alarm in the street interrupted him.

5. 'Revolt of Islam,' canto xii.

www.ingramcontent.com/pod-product-compliance
Lightning Source LLC
Chambersburg PA
CBHW012012110726
47993CB00008B/3028